S0-BAG-551

DATE DUE

Feb 23 '67			
May 22 '67			
Mar 10 80			
Aug 12 '80			
Apr 19 '82			
ORD			PRINTED IN U.S.A.

CHARLES J. "CHUCK" KEENEY is Supervisor of Physical Education at the University of California, Berkeley, where he has been a member of the department staff since 1936. He coached the varsity gymnastics team for twenty years and is Past President of the National Association of Gymnastics Coaches. Mr. Keeney is the author of three books on gymnastics and has contributed articles to *The Modern Gymnast*.

Also by Charles J. Keeney

Elementary Gymnastic Apparatus Skills Illustrated
(with Harold J. Frey)

Trampolining Illustrated

FUNDAMENTAL TUMBLING SKILLS ILLUSTRATED

With Floor Exercise

Charles J. Keeney
University of California, Berkeley

CARL A. RUDISILL LIBRARY
LENOIR RHYNE COLLEGE

THE RONALD PRESS COMPANY · NEW YORK

796.47
K 25 f
56969

Copyright © 1966 by
THE RONALD PRESS COMPANY

_____ Feb. 1967

All Rights Reserved

No part of this book may be reproduced
in any form without permission in writing
from the publisher.

2
VR-B

Library of Congress Catalog Card Number: 66–14162
PRINTED IN THE UNITED STATES OF AMERICA

Dedicated to the often obscure, but necessarily dominant, movement of man toward perfection, in, with, and for his Creator.

Preface

This book has been written for the beginning tumbler and to help the physical education teacher teach the fundamental skills of tumbling and balance. It covers in depth the most important of the basic tumbling skills. In less detail, it covers a considerable number of related skills, variations, and combinations involving the basic skills.

There is a considerable range of difficulty in the stunts presented. The beginner and the instructor of beginners will do well to concentrate on the primary stunts in Chapters 2 and 3, together with a few of the simpler variations and combinations described in connection with them. These ten stunts, learned in approximately the order presented, will be a sufficient challenge to the average high school or college student to fill a series of twenty half-hour lessons. Those with superior talent can, at the same time, learn many of the variations and combinations. In any case, the students should be working on two or three stunts concurrently for variety.

More experienced tumblers will, I am confident, find much helpful material in Chapter 4, not only in the detailed coverage of somersaults and the backward handspring, but also in the key points presented in connection with the variations and combinations described. Aspiring competitive gymnasts in particular will find the material on floor exercise routines in Chapter 5 helpful.

The illustrations are intended to supplement the text and facilitate the acquisition of a mental picture of the skills to be learned. Studying the photographs should not be considered a substitute for careful and thoughtful reading of the text material about each stunt and repeated referral back to it during the course of learning or teaching. The pictures alone say much, but they say much more if used in connection with the word descriptions of the stunts, how to learn them, how to correct them, and how to be safe in the process.

In the preparation of this book I have imposed on the generous natures and talents of several individuals. Mr. John Ostarello of the University of California Physical Education staff has spent many hours behind the camera, utilizing his knowledge of tumbling, his quick finger, and his photographic knowhow to get on film the movements and positions for the illustrations. I am most grateful for this essential assistance.

To the three University of California gymnasts who have cheerfully and skillfully demonstrated the tumbling and floor-exercise stunts for the camera, the reader, and the author, we also owe a debt of gratitude. Art Lloyd has done a fine job of showing his suppleness, which is so important to success in the floor exercise. John Ford, Captain of the University of California 1965 gymnastic team, displays for us some of his many skills in both tumbling and floor exercise. Dan Millman, who in his Freshman and Sophomore years at the University of California has won a World Trampoline Championship and placed high in national collegiate competition in several other events, is our demonstrator for a majority of the tumbling illustrations. Dan is a highly gifted young man with a great past and a greater future in the field of gymnastics. My sincere thanks and best wishes for future success go to these three gymnasts.

CHARLES J. KEENEY

Berkeley, California
January, 1966

Contents

FUNDAMENTAL TUMBLING SKILLS ILLUSTRATED

With Floor Exercise

1

Learning To Tumble

RANGE OF DIFFICULTY

Most of us at one time or another have harbored a wish that we could be "acrobats" and thus be able to balance ourselves upside down and be able to throw our bodies into the air with a variety of gyrations, rotations, twists, flips, and somersaults. Our good sense tells us, however, that the acrobatic heights exemplified by the circus acrobats and the champion tumblers are indeed only achievable by the few who have the physical and mental attributes necessary along with the opportunities, facilities, and instruction, a strong desire, and, in addition, are willing to spend a great deal of time and energy in practice. Tumbling, however, is an activity with a wide range of difficulty. There are tumbling stunts to be learned, bringing pleasure to the learner, which require a minimum of physical prowess, little equipment, and a moderate amount of time and instruction. There are, at the other end of the range, tumbling stunts that can and will be done that no one yet has been able to do.

USE IN COMPETITION

Tumbling has long been one of the events in the sport of competitive gymnastics in the United States. Competitive tumbling is usually done on a continuous strip of mats 5 feet wide, up to 60 feet long, and 2 to 4 inches thick. Sometimes the competition consists of each contestant performing a set series of stunts and being judged on the degree of perfection with which he executes them. Sometimes the competitors are allowed to show whatever stunts or combinations they choose and the judges rate them on difficulty as well as form and style. In other competitions the contestants do some compulsory and some optional work.

Tumbling and balance stunts are also used extensively in another gymnastic event, "Floor Exercise." This is not only an American event, but also an international event and part of Olympic Games Gymnastic Competition. This event is performed on the floor or preferably on a thin mat. The area is approximately 40 feet square and the entire routine, which

3

lasts about 1 minute, is performed within this square. Most of the stunts and variations described in Chapters 2, 3, and 4 in this book are useful in Floor Exercise. Additional description of this event and some examples of Floor Exercise movements and positions not described in the first four chapters will be found in Chapter 5.

PRINCIPLES OF LEARNING

Whether your intentions and ambitions are confined to the lower echelons of tumbling or are fixed on a much higher goal in terms of skill, there has to be a beginning to the learning process and a systematic step-by-step progression from one skill to another. The degree of pleasure experienced from the activity, the safety of the performer, and the steady advancement in tumbling prowess depend on the learning of each stunt and each skill correctly and with fair precision. These principles apply whether the learning is done as a result of self-instruction guided by photographs and the printed word, or from an instructor drawing on his own learning and teaching experiences in addition to authoritative pictorial and instructional references.

NEED FOR EFFECTIVE TEACHING

Too often teaching the fundamentals of tumbling to a class of beginners consists of a demonstration, a few comments, and a "now you do it." Details are ignored, poor style is accepted as normal, and new stunts are introduced in quick succession to "hold interest." Under this system there is a high rate of attrition. Some lose interest immediately because of gross lack of success. Some find little satisfaction in sloppy performance and turn to other activities. Some are discouraged by the minor bumps and injuries resulting from inferior techniques; some come sooner or later to a plateau where the incorrect execution of fundamentals prevents their further advancement. A few of the most talented, most rugged, or the least easily discouraged work their way through these plateaus with a trial-and-error procedure by means of which they correct their faults sufficiently to be able to progress. This "survival of the fittest" manner of teaching often does result in producing some few star tumblers in the long run. More people could make more progress and continue to enjoy tumbling if a more effective method of teaching were employed.

ELEMENTS IN EFFECTIVE TUMBLING INSTRUCTION

PRECISION

One facet of effective teaching and learning in tumbling involves *attention to details*. In this connotation the details are primarily those of correct execution and form. The direction in which the hands are placed; the spatial relations of hands, feet, and head placement; the keeping of legs straight or the timing of their bending are some examples of this kind of detail. Spending time giving the details of execution to the class, watching them closely, correcting the errors, and then repeating instructions frequently can bring great improvement in the group's performance. The class or individual should be frequently reminded of the element of *precision in execution*. Commendation and recognition should be given to individuals who progress beyond the minimum successful performance to a more precise, formful, and graceful execution of the skill. Those who are teaching themselves must be equally insistent on attention to details and precision in execution in their own performance.

PROGRESSIONS

A second characteristic of effective teaching in tumbling is the step-by-step progression in the presentation and learning of skills. This involves not only the learning of the skills in a systematic order but also, in many cases, breaking a stunt down into parts and practicing preparatory actions before attempting the complete skill. Many tumbling stunts can be learned one *part* at a time and later put together into an integrated *whole*. Self-instructors can profit also from attention to progressions and steps in learning.

PRACTICE

Thirdly, effective teaching and learning necessitate space and opportunity for much repetitive practice. During a given instructional or practice session it is important to get as much thoughtful and error-correcting practice as is possible. In a class, this involves, whenever possible, having an individual mat area available for each tumbler, or at least one that he shares with only one other student. Mats can be as small as 3 feet by 5 feet if they are separated from each other by several feet in each direction. Two or three people can work side by side crosswise on a 5 foot by 10 foot mat if it is not too close to another mat. If a large unbroken mat area is shared by the group, each tumbling area should be at least 5 feet by 10 feet. Practicing certain tumbling stunts and series of stunts will, of course, necessitate combining two or more mats for greater space or greater thickness. In these cases two or more tumblers can share the combined mat area by taking alternate practice trys.

The instructor can call the class together into a circular group while he explains and demonstrates the stunt or preparatory exercise he wishes them to practice and then send them to their respective mats for practice. The instructor can then make the rounds giving brief individual help and also admonishing the group from time to time in a louder voice in regard to *general* errors and corrections. The students should be instructed to rest when they feel the need and then resume practice, thus setting their own pace. Practice should be broken every several minutes by a general rest period. During this rest interval the instructor can point out the general faults and give additional pointers and instructions with or without gathering the group into the close instructional formation. With the beginning of each new skill or exercise, when more detailed instructions are appropriate, the group should certainly be called together to better observe and hear the demonstration and instructions.

The self-instructor can apply the same principles by using rest periods to refer back to his pictures and instructions and then, when ready, move on to the next step in progressive learning.

SPOTTING

The final important item in effective teaching of tumbling is the full utilization of mutual physical assistance among the tumblers and, on occasion, between teacher and tumbler. This physical assistance, generally called "spotting," may be simply to add an outside force or balance factor to the performer's own efforts to allow him early in the learning process to go through the complete movement even before he is able to do so completely on his own, and thus speed up learning by giving experience in the integrated movement. This we might call "assistance spotting." The spotting is of even more importance, however, when used for the purpose of protecting the performer from possible injury while he attempts the performance of the stunt. Protective spotting or safety spotting must be a part of any tumbling program that goes beyond the lower elementary level of skill. Tumblers should be trained to spot each other. Such mutual assistance is a socially healthy practice and a procedure that can bring about time economy in a group-teaching and -practice situation. There are, however, from time to time, individuals or stunts that definitely require the spotting services of the strongest and most competent spotter available, which may well be the instructor. Specific spotting instructions and recommendations will be found in the following chapters along with the descriptions and other information about each specific skill.

2

Rolls and Balances

Stunt No. 1—FORWARD ROLL

DESCRIPTION OF ACTION

From a standing position bend your knees completely and at the same time lean forward and reach both arms forward toward two points, shoulder width apart, on the mat a yard or so forward of your feet (Fig. 1A). As you complete your knee bend and before your hands come to their landing spots, you start straightening your legs. As the knees become straight and the hands come to the mat (Fig. 1B), the arms bend and the head is ducked down to a chin-on-chest position. After the feet leave the mat, the back of the head comes to rest on the mat at a point slightly beyond the hands. You roll in this bent-body straight-knee, pointed-foot position onto the shoulders (Fig. 1C). As the roll continues onto the back, the knees start to bend and come closer to the chest, the hands leave the mat and come to grasping positions on the shins. As you roll on up onto your seat, you bend your arms to pull your tucked legs in closer (Fig. 1D). You continue rolling onto your feet, release the grip on your shins, and stand up.

STEPS IN LEARNING

1. Lie on your back, bend your knees, grasp your shins a little above the mid-point between knees and ankles, lift your head forward dropping your chin to your chest. This makes your backside rounded like a rocker on a rocking chair. Start rocking back and forth from a momentary balance on your shoulders and neck to a tucked sit-up and return. By opening your tuck position while on the neck (Fig. 1E) and closing it tightly while rocking forward, you will be able to get enough rocking momentum to come to a momentary balance on the feet with the seat off the mat before you rock back again onto the seat, back, and then shoulders. This exercise is called the rocking tuck.
2. From a squat position with the hands on the mat about 24 inches forward of the feet (Fig. 1F), straighten both knees and rise up to the tiptoes. While doing this, keep the arms straight and continue to look at the mat between your hands (Fig. 1G). Bend your knees again returning to the

7

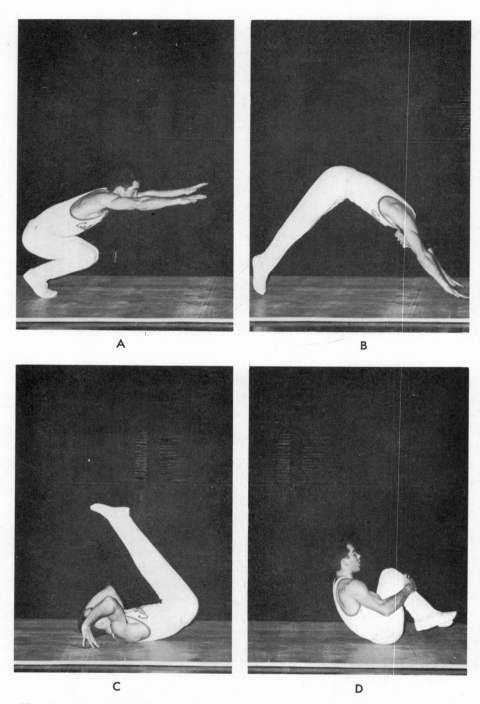

Fig. 1. Forward Roll. A. The squat-and-reach start, leaning forward. B. The leg drive. C. The pretuck roll onto the back. D. The tucked roll up to a stand.

Fig. 1E. The rocking tuck, open portion.

Fig. 1F. Squat start of Step 2 of learning procedure.

Fig. 1G. Hips-high position for Step 2 of learning procedure.

Fig. 1H. Hips-high, head-down position for Step 3 of learning procedure.

squat position sitting on your heels. Repeat this exercise a number of times.

3. Repeat Step 2 with these differences. At the same time the legs are being straightened, bend your arms and drop your chin down to your chest until you are touching the back of your head to the mat between your hands and have your knees straight (Fig. 1H). Return to your starting position and repeat the exercise. If your arms are not strong enough to support the weight and thus allow you just to lightly touch the back of the head to the mat, you must substitute an inferior position wherein you rest your weight on the top of the head on the mat between your hands. This is not as good because it does not teach you to turn your head under as far as you should.

4. If you go through Step 3 with more force and speed, straightening your knees more abruptly, you will find yourself rolling over onto the back of your neck and shoulders. Keep your knees straight and your body bent and roll on over into a straight-legged sitting position. Make sure on this exercise that you put the back of your head firmly on the mat beyond your hands, and that you keep the knees straight and feet pointed all the way to the sit-up finish.

5. By combining the first part of Step 4 with the technique learned in Step 1, you will have an almost complete roll. Start then as you did in Step 4 and when you are rolling across your shoulders with your knees straight, change to the tuck position, grasping the shins, roll to the momentary balance on your feet in a squat position, release your hands from the shins, and stand up. The speed of the change from the straight-knee form to the tuck must be paced with the rest of the roll. If you are rolling over slowly, do not make the change abruptly.

6. The final step in this progression toward the completed forward roll starts from a balance squat position with the hands off the mat but reaching out toward their proper place, about 1 yard ahead of the feet. Lean forward from this position and start the knee-straightening action. As the hands land on the mat, the arms take their bend, the head is ducked under, and the feet leave the mat. From here on proceed as in the latter portion of Step 5. When you are successful at doing this roll smoothly and with good form, then you are ready to do the whole stunt from a standing start as described above under the heading "Description of Action."

CORRECTION OF ERRORS

A. The common errors to look for are: 1) failure to straighten the legs completely before the tuck; 2) putting the hands down too close to the feet; 3) ducking the head down too soon; 4) putting the head down closer to the feet than the line where the hands are placed; 5) putting the top of the head to the mat; 6) turning the head under so far or holding the arms too straight too long so that the head does not come firmly to the mat before the shoulders land; 7) not grasping the shins at the right place; 8) changing from straight knee to tuck too soon, too late, too abruptly, or too slowly to be smooth; and 9) coming to a stand by pushing the hands against the mat instead of grasping the shins.

B. To detect and correct the above-listed errors refer to the descriptions of the correct form in the "Description of Action" and in the "Steps in Learning" as well as to the illustrations. Repeating the learning steps until each one is done consistently correctly is the best method of avoiding or correcting errors in the completed stunt.

VARIATIONS AND COMBINATIONS

1.1. Series of Forward Rolls.   To go from one forward roll to another do not stand up after the first but instead stay in the squat, lean immediately forward, and reach out and look forward to the mat a yard or so ahead as you straighten your knees to start the next roll. The series should be done moderately fast but not so fast as to lose the correct form.

1.2. Roll Down from Handstand.   After you have learned to kick up to and hold a momentary handstand (Stunt No. 4), you may wish to use the roll as a means of coming to your feet again or of saving yourself when you inadvertently overturn the balance. To roll down from the handstand, first overbalance, then bend the arms and place the back of the head on the mat forward of the hands (Fig. 1.2). Roll to the shoulders and back, bending at the knees and at the waist. Take the hands from the mat to the shins, completing the tuck. Roll to a squat balance and then stand.

Fig. 1.2.   Roll-down from handstand.

Fig. 1.3. Straight-knee rise from forward roll.

1.3. Straight-Knee Rise from Forward Roll. The essential difference between this stunt and the orthodox forward roll is the absence of any tuck or knee bend in the latter part of the stunt. The recovery to the feet is done by rolling through the straight-knee sitting position and pushing down vigorously with the hands on the mat beside the thighs. You must carry good momentum through the roll and bend forward extremely at the waist while pushing with the hands in order to get up to a stand (Fig. 1.3). The straight-knee getup can be done from the handstand roll down (Stunt No. 1.2) also. When done from the handstand, sufficient momentum can be gained by leaning a long time before bending the arms, by putting the back of the head down farther forward than normal, and by keeping the body straight as long as possible before bending at the waist. The straight-knee finish can also be done with legs spread wide and with hand-push between the legs to a straddle stand.

Stunt No. 2—BACKWARD ROLL

DESCRIPTION OF ACTION

As in the forward roll you start this stunt from a standing position with the first motion being a deep knee bend. The squatting action is accompanied by a backward lean (Fig. 2A). The combination results in a sitting contact with the mat that progresses to a rolling on the rounded back toward the shoulders. As the shoulders and back of the head make contact

Fig. 2. Backward Roll. A. Tucked sit-down for backward roll. B. Halfway over. C. The push of the arms. D. Coming up to a stand.

with the mat, the body is kept doubled up tightly with the knees against the chest, the knees bent as far as possible, and the chin tucked down against the chest between the knees. At this stage of the roll the hands are placed back behind or beside the shoulders at least shoulder width apart with the palms down flat on the mat and with the fingers pointing sideward (Fig. 2B). As the body weight comes to rest on the shoulders and back of the head, you push down with your hands as forcefully as you can to lift the doubled-up body off the mat so that the backward rotation can continue without putting undue pressure on the neck (Fig. 2C). As you turn on over backward you come to rest on your feet in a deep-squat position with your hands still on the mat. Straightening up to a stand completes the stunt (Fig. 2D).

STEPS IN LEARNING

1. Lie down on your back on the mat with your arms on the mat alongside of you. Draw your knees up to your shoulders and bend the knees as far as you can. Put your hands back beside the shoulders with the palms down and the fingers turned out. You may need someone to hold you in balance to maintain this position. This is the halfway-over position for a backward roll (Fig. 2B).
2. From a sitting position on the mat with your doubled-up legs against your chest, your head down between your knees, and your hands in a palms-up, turned-out position beside your shoulders, roll back to the halfway-over position described in Step 1. Return to the sitting-up position and repeat a number of times.
3. Get an assistant to help you turn over backward from the static halfway position to the squat landing on your feet by lifting you under the hips and rotating you backward as you push with your hands (Fig. 2E). Don't kick out or open out as you are being turned over. It is not only the

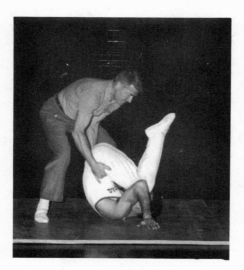

Fig. 2E. Assistance spotting for the beginner.

wrong way to do this particular style of backward roll, but it can be pretty hard on your helper.

4. After you have been helped over a few times from the static halfway position, you can ask your helper to step in and boost you over when you reach the halfway-over position as you are rolling back from a sit as in Step 2.

5. Now, if you add the momentum of the sitting down with a backward-lean action to the first part of the roll, you will probably be able to push yourself over onto your feet without any outside assistance.

CORRECTION OF ERRORS

A. The most common cause of failure to get over and of crooked turnovers is the placing of the hands in a position too close to the head and in a manner that prevents an effective push at the right moment. The use of the wide, fingers-pointing-outward position for the hand placement and the emphasis on the hand and arm push at the earliest possible moment are the corrections for this error.

B. Turning the head to one side instead of bending it straight downward is a direct cause of crookedness but is itself a result of poor hand placement, lack of push, or lack of momentum. Even after the causes are corrected, the crooked head may persist from habit. Trying to turn it in the opposite direction may help overcome the habit.

C. Kicking out or opening up during the roll is a deviation from the tucked form specified for this stunt. There are some variations of the backward roll that include such an opening action.

VARIATIONS AND COMBINATIONS

2.1. A Series of Backward Rolls. If another backward roll is to follow the first, you do not stand up after the first roll but instead use your hands to push you backward in the squat position into the next roll (Fig. 2.1).

Fig. 2.1. Between rolls of a series.

The stand-up is done at the end of the series. Three or four fast backward rolls in succession may make you a little dizzy and thereby complicate the standing-up attempt at the end.

2.2. Backward Roll Extension. During the early part of the backward roll you start opening a little bit from the tuck and about the time the hands come to the mat you open up forcefully extending your feet toward the ceiling (Fig. 2.2), pushing down with the hands to straighten the arms, and raising the head. This puts you into a momentary handstand (Fig. 4D). From the handstand you can double up again bringing your feet down to the mat by your hands from which position you can stand or start another roll. A more advanced technique is to snap down from the handstand as in the handstand jerk described later in this chapter (Stunt No. 4.1).

Fig. 2.2. Pushing toward a backward roll extension.

2.3. Straight-Knee Backward Rolls. The knees may be kept straight instead of being bent for the sit-down start and/or during the remainder of the roll. To sit smoothly and softly without bending the knees it is necessary to bend extremely forward at the waist and reach downward and backward with both arms past the legs to make contact with the floor with the hands, well before the back sides of the legs reach the floor (Fig. 2.3). After the arms have eased the legs to the floor, there is an immediate opening action at the waist as the upper body swings back toward a supine position and the hands reach back to their position near the shoulders. The legs are then raised to the tuck as in previously described backward rolls or into

Fig. 2.3. Sitting into a straight-knee backward roll.

a pike position if the knees are to remain straight throughout the roll. If the legs remain straight, they may continue in the pike position while the arms push you over onto your feet; they may spread wide apart but still maintain the pike bend at the waist; or they may swing vigorously in a vertical direction opening you up from the waist into an inverted straight body support on the hands (momentary handstand). The handstand may be followed by either a snap down (Stunt No. 4.1) or simply a pike down, bending at the waist again but not at the knees, bringing the feet to the floor before the hands are picked up.

Stunt No. 3—HEADSTAND

DESCRIPTION OF ACTION

Kneel down and place the hands on the mat in front of your knees at a distance apart a little greater than your shoulder width. The hands should point forward-outward about halfway between straight ahead and straight to the side, and should be placed palm downward. Now bend forward and place the *top* of the head on the mat well forward of the hands so that the hands and head are resting upon the points of a triangle of approximately equal sides. Raise your knees from the mat so that you are resting only on your hands, head, and feet. Walk forward with your feet until they are as close up toward your hands as you can comfortably bring them without

Fig. 3. Headstand. A. Knees on top of arms; the frog headstand. B. Knees lifted off; the tucked headstand. C. Knees away from chest but still fully bent. D. The objective reached; straight headstand.

losing the top-of-the-head supporting position. At this time and during the remaining movements the elbows should be bent at right angles with the elbow directly over the hand. This will require a little conscious effort to pull the elbows closer together than their natural position.

Next, pick up one foot, bend the knee as far as you can, and place the knee on top of the upper arm near the elbow. Do the same with the other knee, increasing the amount of push exerted by the arms. This should put you into the frog headstand (Fig. 3A), which is also called the three-legged stool or the squat headstand. From the frog headstand push a little harder with the hands, raise the knees from the elbows, and bring the tightly bent knees closer to your chest to a tucked headstand (Fig. 3B). The next move is to start opening at the waist, taking the knees away from the chest but not at once unbending at the knee (Fig. 3C). When a fairly open position has been achieved at the waist, then the legs are straightened upward to the headstand position. As you proceed from the tucked headstand to this final position, the push with the arms must be gradually lessened to avoid overbalancing. The final position is with body straight or very slightly arched (hyperextended) and with the knees straight, feet pointed and together (Fig. 3D).

STEPS IN LEARNING

1. Follow the description of action above as far as the frog headstand. Check this position for correct placement of head, hands, elbows, and knees. Return to beginning position and rest. Repeat a number of times until facility is acquired.
2. Now, from the frog headstand, practice lifting the knees and closing tight to the tucked headstand described above. Open from the tuck with the bent knee but straightening-at-the-waist action. Stop here, come back down, and repeat a few times.
3. Work with a partner who stands beside you and helps you to avoid falling by catching your legs as you try the final opening-out action into the straight headstand. Soon you will feel sufficiently confident to try it without your "spotter" (assistant).

CORRECTIONS OF ERRORS

A. Resting the weight on the forehead or forepart of the top of the head is a mistake. It puts too much strain on the neck and too much weight on the arms. The top of the head position permits the weight to be supported easily and comfortably by the straight neck and leaves only a small balancing weight on the hands.
B. Another common error is the failure to place the head far enough forward of the hands. A shallow triangle is not as efficient a base for balance as is the equilateral triangle.
C. Other errors frequently noticeable are failure to keep the elbows inward

over the hands, turning the hands in the wrong direction, opening the legs from the tuck before rotating the hips so the opening will be vertical, a too strong and too prolonged push with the hands as the headstand position is reached, and too much body arch in the final headstand position.

VARIATIONS AND COMBINATIONS

3.1. The Tuck Press-Up to Headstand.   The close tuck position of the legs is assumed while the feet are still on the mat.   By pressing with the hands and without losing the tuck, the feet are raised off of the mat (Fig. 3.1). The frog position is thus eliminated, but the tuck is unfolded into the straight headstand as in the frog press to headstand.

Fig. 3.1. Going directly to the tucked press without the frog position.

Fig. 3.2. The leg lifts in a gentle kickup to headstand.

3.2. The Kickup to Headstand.   Place the hands and head on the mat and work the feet up as close as possible with straight knees. Push with the arms, lift one leg up backward as high as you can into a split-type position keeping the knee straight (Fig. 3.2). As this kickup leg reaches its height, you jump a little from the foot that is still on the mat and lift it up with straight knee to join the kickup leg in the straight headstand position (Fig. 4D).

Fig. 3.3. Pressing to headstand; jackknife style.

Fig. 3.4. Forearm-and-head headstand.

3.3 Jackknife Press to Headstand. From a position with hands and head properly placed on mat and body bent so that with straight legs the toes are resting on the mat as close up to the hands as possible, you push very hard with the arms, raise the toes off the mat (Fig. 3.3), and continue unbending at the waist to the straight headstand. The arm pressure must diminish gradually as the body opens and the final position is approached.

3.4. Forearm and Head Headstand. Place the forearms on the mat with the elbows wide apart and the hands together so that they form an inverted V with about a 90° angle inside the point of the V. The fingers of the hands should be overlapping or intertwined and the palms should be tipped somewhat upward. Place the top of the head on the mat so that the back of the head is against the palms of your hands. Walk up close with your feet and then lift your legs up into the headstand by means of the tuck press-up or the kickup as described above for headstand variations 3.1 and 3.2. The final headstand position is straight, not arched, and the balance is carried on the forearms and top of the head (Fig. 3.4).

3.5. Backward Roll to Headstand. Start the backward roll (see Stunt No. 2) and as you roll onto your back, start gradually straightening out at the waist and knees so that after you have rolled onto the back of your neck and are rolling to the top of your head, you have straightened out com-

Fig. 3.5. Just before hand placement in a backward roll to headstand.

pletely with your feet pointing straight upward. To maintain this position in balance you must get the hands and head immediately into the triangular relationship shown in Fig. 3D. This can be accomplished in any one of three ways. You may use the hands as you do in an ordinary backward roll until you roll to the top of the head and then quickly move the hands into the triangle formation. The same results can be obtained by a similar start but instead of moving the hands the weight is taken onto the hands and the head is moved forward. The third method is really the best. It involves doing the early part of the roll onto the back of the neck and onto the head without placing the hands on the mat, and then placing them quickly and firmly in their triangular positions as you get to the extended positions on the top of your head (Fig. 3.5).

Stunt No. 4—KICKUP TO MOMENTARY HANDSTAND

DESCRIPTION OF ACTION

From a standing position with one foot forward of the other, lift the arms into a forward-reaching position about shoulder width apart. Support your weight almost entirely on the forward leg with the toe of the other foot in light contact with the floor to the rear (Fig. 4A). Bend forward at your waist and place your hands on the mat 20 to 30 inches ahead of the forward foot with the index fingers pointing straight ahead and the other fingers spread as far as possible (Fig. 4B). As your hands are first coming into

Fig. 4. Kickup to Momentary Handstand. A. Starting stance. B. Just before the back-leg swing-up. C. Coming toward the vertical; still in partial splits. D. The near-balance momentary handstand.

contact with the mat, you swing your straight back leg up behind you with moderate force and, at the same time, spring from the forward leg by straightening the knee and pressing away with the foot. As your back (kickup) leg reaches the near-vertical position (Fig. 4C), the forward (jumping) leg is swung up beside it and the straight-body, straight-leg inverted position of the momentary handstand has been reached (Fig. 4D). During the whole procedure the head will hold the correct upward position if you keep looking approximatley at the spot on the mat forward of your hands where your head would be on a headstand.

If the kickup has been with the right amount of force, you can, by pressing downward with your fingers, check the forward rotating force and begin the return trip. As you start falling toward the frontside downward position from which you started, you should bend sharply at the waist splitting the legs apart to reach one foot toward the mat close to the hands, bending that leg as little as possible. The weight should be taken onto that foot and the hands lifted from the mat before the other foot comes to the mat.

STEPS IN LEARNING

1. Learning the headstand, especially the kickup to headstand, will help you to learn the handstand.
2. Take a position on the mat similar to a sprinter's "set" position with the hands on the mat and one leg forward and bent, the other reaching backward with straight knee, and with the foot touching the mat. The hands are shoulder width apart, 20 to 30 inches forward of the front foot. The arms are straight, the shoulders over the hands, and the eyes are looking at the mat between and forward of the hands. Without letting the arms bend or the shoulders move forward, lift the back leg (straight knee) up high behind and spring a little from the front foot. The front foot should leave the mat briefly and return to the same spot. During this arm-supported interval, the legs remain in a maximum split position as if trying to point the kickup leg at the ceiling while pointing the jumping leg at the mat. This split-type momentary handstand should be practiced with gradually increasing force up to the point where the near-balance position is attained and maintained for a few seconds before returning to the landing foot.
3. The next step requires the help of a partner. The performer takes the same position as in beginning Step 2 above. The helper stands *beside* the performer. After the performer executes the kickup as in Step 2, the helper grasps the high leg moving it to, and holding it in, the vertical position while the performer raises the jumping leg up beside it, closing the split position. This partner-supported handstand is held for about 5 seconds and then the helper releases the performer so that his balance is moving in the right direction so that he can sharply and widely split his legs apart again and make his landing as in Step 2.
4. The partner-catch system used in Step 3 is also useful to help learn the kickup from a standing start. The performer follows the instructions to

be found above in the first part of the "Description of Action," while the helper stands beside him to catch his kickup leg when vertical to prevent overturning. When the performer is fairly proficient, the helper can, instead of grasping the leg, simply put his arm up to act as a block to prevent overturning. The performer may rest his legs against the outstretched arm of his partner until he is ready to come down, and then by splitting his legs, he can send his own balance back toward his landing.

5. Learning to use the wall as a partner will facilitate practice and speed up learning. The hands should be placed from 12 to 18 inches from the wall on the mat or floor. Care should be taken to keep the shoulders from moving forward, the arms from bending, and the eyes focused on the floor about the spot where it meets the wall. In kicking up, either from the "set" position or from a stand, there should be an attempt to kick and jump just enough to come to a momentary balance. If the kickup is a little too strong, the wall will catch the feet. If the kickup is just right or too weak, the wall will not be needed. Even when intending to go against the wall, don't bend the knees and reach for it, keep the knees straight and wait until the feet come to the wall by necessity. Coming down from the wall, practice the sharp, wide split and the straight-leg close-in landing.

6. Before trying the completed stunt without partner and without wall, it is necessary to learn how to save yourself when you overturn. For this learning procedure it is well to use a partner to help you hold the handstand position while you get organized for your overturn. When your helper lets you go in an overturning balance, you shift your weight onto one hand, turn about 90° toward the hand you leave down, step forward and around with the hand you picked up, and, at the same time, bend at the waist to bring your foot or feet down to the mat. You can acquire the ability to shift to one hand by trying it while being supported by the wall. This is a sort of an emergency saving action and is not meant to be particularly graceful, but primarily to keep you from falling onto your back when you accidentally overturn.

7. Now you should be ready to do it alone trying to lift the leg and spring with just the amount of force necessary to acquire the near-vertical position and not with so much force that you cannot, by pressing with the fingers, keep from overturning and return the way you came up. If you cannot prevent the overturn, use the twisting emergency landing you have learned in Step 6.

CORRECTION OF ERRORS

A. Inability to support the weight is not usually due to a disparity between strength and body size but may be. Usually the collapsing of the arms is due rather to letting the shoulders get forward out of line, letting the arms bend at the elbow, having the head down, or having the hands too close together.

B. Errors of position spoil the appearance and to some extent decrease the steadiness of the momentary handstand. The handstand position should be fairly rigid, straight, or slightly arched (hyperextended) at the waist, straight legged and with pointed feet. These positions can be learned lying front side down (prone) on the mat. They can be practiced in the headstand, and in the partner-supported and wall-supported handstands. In the independent, momentary handstand be sure that at the peak of the balance the legs are closed and all the bend is removed from the waist-hip area.

C. In the twisting-overturn-save, difficulty is often caused by trying to bend at the waist and bring the feet down without first turning and stepping forward with one hand, or by taking the turn and step when not actually overbalanced. Correction of these errors may require a return to partner assistance (as in Step 6) so that a thoughtful organized effort can be made to turn, step, and bend correctly to make a smooth comfortable save instead of a fall.

VARIATIONS AND COMBINATIONS

4.1. Handstand Jerk. While in the momentary handstand, let the knees bend to about a right angle, increase the arch in the back, let the elbows bend slightly, and start falling from balance toward the front side down position (Fig. 4.1). When about 45° from the vertical, forcefully straighten your knees and immediately bend as much and as fast as possible at the waist. At the same time you push away from the mat with your hands by straightening your elbows and pressing down with your fingers. The total of these forceful actions should bring you to a standing position with a slight forward bend at the waist. The knee straightening just before and

Fig. 4.1. Ready for the kick, bend, and push of the handstand jerk.

with the bending at the waist is most important. Bending at the waist before or without straightening the knees will not bring the snap action, so essential to success.

4.2. Donkey Kicks. From a momentary handstand, execute handstand jerk (Stunt No. 4.1), land on the ball of the feet leaning forward (Fig. 4.2), and immediately bounce off the feet dropping the hands back toward the mat and lifting the hips up behind in a jackknife action. As the hands come to the floor, the body is straightening out of the jackknife to the handstand position. This landing is somewhat short of the vertical balance and, even while landing, it is necessary to acquire the arched-back, bent-knee, off-balance position leading to another jerk. The knees are not bent as much on the handstand landing as on the initial handstand. Each jerk is followed by another bounce off the feet onto the hands and this continues as long as desired. The resemblance to a bucking animal has given this stunt its name. This is more of a fun stunt than a competitive one.

4.3. Moving Handbalance. After kicking up to a momentary handstand, you start shifting your weight back and forth from hand to hand without bending your arms. Each time you pick up your hand an inch or so off the mat as you rock onto the other arm and set it down again a little forward or a little backward of its former place, depending on which way you are falling at the moment. Having the hands turned fingers outward is a helpful practice (Fig. 4.3). The objective is to remain in the handbalance,

Fig. 4.2. Landing and bouncing between "donkey kicks."

Fig. 4.3. Moving handbalance.

rocking back and forth like a man on stilts, shifting the hands almost automatically to be under the balance each time they come down. The rocking is continuous and regular. The shifting back and forth can first be learned while leaning the feet against the wall. Endurance contests in this moving handbalance are challenging and developmental.

4.4. Handwalk. This is similar to Variation No. 4.3 except that the steps are larger and continue in one direction. For forward walking you wait until the balance is overturned, then, shifting the weight to one arm, step forward with the other to a point almost, but not quite, under the overturning balance (Fig. 4.4). The weight shifts immediately to this forward-

Fig. 4.4. Handwalking, just after a forward step with the left hand.

stepping arm while the balance continues to overturn. The free arm is then swung forward of the supporting one and the weight is shifted to it so that a walking forward action is continued. A continuous overbalance is necessary to make possible continuous forward walking. The hands turned out to the sides position may help in keeping arms straight and in shifting the balance. Backward walking, sideward stepping, circling, and even dance steps are possible to those willing to do the required amount of practicing. Walking-for-distance contests can build interest and muscles.

4.5. Handbalance. To stand in one place on one's hands and maintain balance for a considerable time (10 seconds or more) is more difficult in terms of learning time than the moving handbalance (Stunt No. 4.3) or the handwalk (Stunt No. 4.4). The hands must be in the spread-fingered posi-

Fig. 4.5. Correct position for a stationary handstand.

tion with the index fingers pointing forward. The balancing is done almost exclusively by means of downward pressure against the mat exerted by the ten fingers. Many balancers find that they can exert more pressure by raising the middle-joint of each finger, leaving the end joint and the palm of the hand on the mat (Fig. 4.5). To exert the right amount of pressure to prevent overturn and still not force the balance back onto the palm and heel of the hand is the necessary skill that takes time and practice and patience to learn. A correctly balanced handbalance is always a little over-balanced, leaning on the leverage of the fingers, but never underbalanced where there are no fingers to exert holding pressure. Using the wall to support the feet and balancing away from this support by means of finger pressure and the slow moving of one foot away from the wall are big helps in learning to balance. Do not shift the shoulders out of their over-the-hands position in order to get the feet off the wall. Standing still and steady on the hands for 1 minute is a major accomplishment.

Stunt No. 5—DIVE AND ROLL

DESCRIPTION OF ACTION

From a run, jump forward with a low gliding jump from one foot to two. During this jump, which is more properly called a hurdle because of its similarity to the springboard diver's hurdle, the legs remain at full exten-

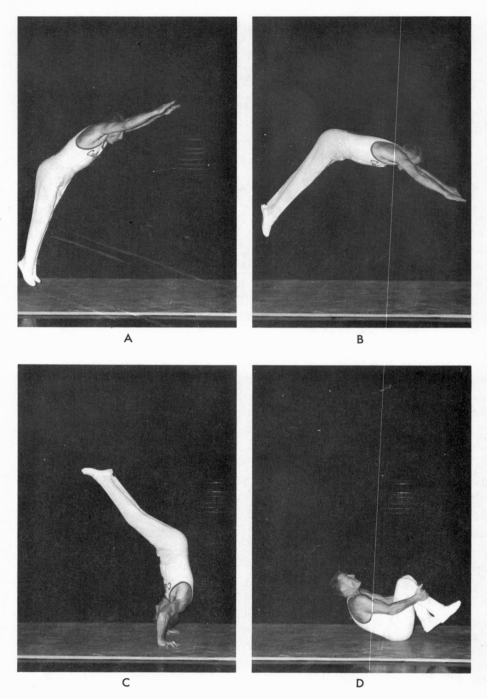

Fig. 5.   Dive and Roll.   A. Immediately after the takeoff in reach-type dive and roll.   B. About midway in the flight.   C. After landing; beginning the roll. D. The tucked roll moving toward the stand-up finish.

sion without drawing up the knees. The arms are raised forward upward to a reaching forward position during the hurdle and the upper body moves forward a little more than the feet. As you land on the balls of both feet, you are leaning somewhat forward and your arms are already reaching forward toward your next landing spot. You immediately bounce off the balls of your feet reaching forward and looking at the mat at a point 5 to 10 feet forward of your takeoff line (Fig. 5A). This distance will depend on the length of your dive, which in turn depends on the speed of your run and the force of your jump. As you leave the mat, you stretch out into a horizontal straight-leg position (Fig. 5B). As you rotate forward, your hands come to the mat and your arms are allowed to bend with muscular resistance to absorb some of the shock. Your head is turned down, chin-to-chest, to allow the back of the head to come to the mat with moderate force at a point between the hand placement (Fig. 5C). As these landings are being made, you bend forward somewhat to round off the back. Now the shoulders and the back make contact in rolling succession. The body is bent more at the waist, but the knees remain relatively straight until you have rolled onto your shoulders. At this point bend the knees, grasp your shins, and roll in this tuck position (Fig. 5D) to your feet and stand up.

STEPS IN LEARNING

1. The forward roll (Stunt No. 1) should have been learned and well practiced with the straight-knee to tuck form suggested before trying to learn the dive and roll.
2. The extended or reaching forward roll should be the next step. From a squat start, as for an ordinary forward roll, reach out as far as possible to do your roll. More spring with the legs will be necessary to carry you through when you reach farther.
3. The standing dive and roll from the squat start will be the next logical step. When you begin reaching so far in the reaching forward roll that your leg spring precedes the hand placement and the feet leave the mat before the hands land, you are doing a dive and roll.
4. The standing dive and roll from a stand-up takeoff without the squat start should soon be substituted. To start this stunt, stand with arms extended forward and bend slightly forward at the waist. Keeping the knees straight, start falling forward off balance. After leaning about 20°, quickly bend your knees slightly and quickly straighten them again springing from your feet into your dive. Keep your knees straight, your arms reaching, and your eyes on the landing area during your flight (as in Figs. 5A and 5B). Land on the hands, back of the head, and shoulders, rolling onto the shoulders with straight knees. Bend the knees, grasp the shins, and roll to the feet, then stand up. Work for a good, smooth, straight-knee, standing dive roll about 5 feet long before you begin to learn the running dive.
5. A forward jump to a dive and roll is a good stepping stone between the standing dive and roll and the running dive and roll. At first raise the

arms to the reaching position before jumping. Later, they should be raised during the jump, but they should be in the forward reach for the dive takeoff. The forward jump is from two feet to two feet. The jump landing is on the balls of the feet with a forward body lean so that the nearly straight-knee, bouncing takeoff into the dive can follow immediately.

6. A single step and hurdle into the dive and then several walking steps before the hurdle and dive are useful preliminaries to the running dive and roll. In both of these the arms are swung into the forward reach position during the hurdle. The walking approach can be converted gradually into a run.

CORRECTION OF ERRORS

A. Failure to make a smooth landing and roll up to the feet is most often the result of not keeping the legs straight during the flight and the first part of the roll. If the knees are bent too soon from carelessness or a premature attempt to start the tuck, the landing is apt to be overturned and bumpy.

B. Another cause of overturning is a failure to reach out far enough forward for the landing. The length of the dive must be commensurate with the force of the jump. If the hands are put down at a distance of 4 feet for what should have been a 6 foot long dive, the body will slam down to the mats beyond the hands instead of rolling smoothly and under control into the tuck.

C. Failure to watch the mat at the landing area until about the time the hands land; failure to slow down the landing force with the arm resistance; ducking the head too hard and too far and thereby missing the mat entirely with the head, or putting the head down closer to the point of takeoff than the hands land: These are all errors leading to bumpy landings.

D. Most common errors at the takeoff are the use of the squat and jump takeoff instead of the bounce, and the failure to have the arms in the forward reach position by the time you land on two feet for the dive takeoff.

VARIATIONS AND COMBINATIONS

5.1. Upswing Dive and Roll. The primary difference between this stunt and the running dive and roll (Stunt No. 5) previously described is, as the name implies, a matter of a different arm swing. For this dive the arms are swung to a position downward and backward during the first part of the hurdle and then swing forward and upward with the takeoff drive from the two feet. The takeoff tends to be less of a bounce off the balls of the feet and more of a quick spring off the whole foot with a press away to a pointed foot. The effect adds to the lifting force and thereby increases the distance and height potentials of the dive. It also makes the dive a bit more difficult to control and to do smoothly and in good form. It should be learned after the ordinary running dive and roll and should be tried on a small scale and gradually increased to full effort attempts.

5.2. Backswing Dive and Roll (Russian Dive). Still another type of arm swing for a dive and roll is the downward and backward swing. During the early part of the hurdle the arms are lifted to a forward reaching position; then just before the hurdle landing on two feet, the arms start their full sweep swing downward and backward so that they reach their high point behind the body as the tumbler takes off from the mat into his dive (Fig. 5.2). Needless to say, the arms must swing forward again to lead the dive to the hands-first landing and roll. The foot placement after the hurdle before the dive is even more flat-footed than that for the upswing dive (Stunt No. 5B); the knees bend a little more and the feet are on the mat a little longer. The takeoff spring is a press-away type of drive and depends for its effectiveness not so much on the speed of the run and hurdle as on the exactly timed lifting force of the vigorous arm sweep. The body is lifted partially by the transference of this arm-swing force to the body as the arms are abruptly stopped at the end of their back swing. This is a good dive for getting good height from a short run, but is not good for distance diving. Considerable practice will be necessary before the arm action can be timed correctly with the other actions. The standing backswing dive and roll is a good trick in itself and a good preparation for the running one.

Fig. 5.2. Backswing (Russian) dive takeoff.

Fig. 5.3. Swan dive during flight.

5.3. Swan Dive and Roll. The swan position during the flight of the dive involves the lifted head, the outstretched arms, the slightly arched (hyperextended) body line, and the straight, closed legs with pointed feet (Fig. 5.3). The takeoff action and arm swing may be any of the three described in the description of Stunts 5, 5.1, and 5.2. The upswing takeoff is probably the most effective start for the swan dive. The key to correct body position is the tightened leg and buttocks muscles. The ordinary dive should be very well learned before attempting the swan. The sideward extension of the arms should be added only after the body position has been mastered. This is a spectacular stunt when well done.

5.4. Dive to Straight-Knee Roll-Up. The straight knee getup as described for Stunt No. 1.3 with legs extended or widespread can be used with great effectiveness instead of the usual tucked roll after any of the above dives. In order to be able to apply the techniques described for Stunt No. 1.3 to the dive roll, it is necessary to have the landing of the dive smooth and well controlled. The types of dives that are most easily controlled are, therefore, the best for this purpose. The standing dive and roll with the reaching form (Stunt No. 5, Learning Step 4) and the backswing dive and roll (Stunt No. 5.2) either standing or running are the best for this purpose. This stunt, as well as many others described in this book, is effectively used in Floor Exercise routines.

3

Cartwheel, Snap Up, and Related Skills

Stunt No. 6—CARTWHEEL

DESCRIPTION OF ACTION

From a standing position raise both arms forward upward overhead and at the same time swing one foot forward (Fig. 6A). Lean forward immediately and take a forward step 24 to 36 inches long while lowering the arms toward the mat and bending forward at the waist. Place the hand corresponding to the forward foot on the mat a yard or so ahead of the foot with the fingers pointing to the side of the mat. At the moment the hand comes to the mat, you swing your back leg (right) up behind without bending the knee and spring from the forward leg (left) by straightening the knee and pressing away with the foot (Fig. 6B). This sends you through a momentary support on one hand with legs spread wide and bent at the waist. As the balance moves forward over this hand, the body pivots somewhat, following the lead of the sideward-turned hand on the mat. Soon the other hand (right) is placed on the mat about 24 inches beyond and facing the same direction as the first hand and the body pivot continues (Fig. 6C). The hands should both be on a straight line with the spot where the takeoff foot was placed and this line extends in the direction of the original facing. The balance is carried briefly on both hands with legs split laterally as the forward flexion at the hips is straightened out. The moving balance shifts next onto the second hand and the first hand is lifted off the mat. The body continues to pivot past the sideward facing 90° turn and on toward the 180° turn. When the weight is balanced over the second hand and moving on past, you flex again at the waist bringing the kickup leg down sharply to a straight-knee landing close to the second hand, on the same imaginary line on which the takeoff foot and both hands have been placed and with the foot facing the hand (Fig. 6D). Pick up the hand that is still

Fig. 6. Cartwheel. A. Starting position. B. After the kickup during the first quarter turn. C. Riding to the far hand. D. The sharp cut-down to landing leg.

on the mat (right) and straighten up to a standing position. Set the other foot down apart from but in line with the landing foot coming to a stand with legs split facing back where you came from, with one leg behind the other or pivot to face sideward with legs spread laterally.

STEPS IN LEARNING

1. Practice the kickup to momentary handstand (Stunt No. 4) coming down first onto the leg that went up first (right, for example). The kickup should be srong enough to allow the complete straightening of the body in the handstand but still be a little short of vertical balance so that the comedown follows immediately after the kickup. The legs should be kept straight, the split should be wide, and the landing foot (right) should come down close to the hands (right). The shoulders should be kept less far forward than for an ordinary handstand.

2. Do the same exercise as in Step 1 except that you place the hands on the mat one at a time and pick them up one at a time. The sequence is as follows. As you swing the back foot (right) up, you place the opposite hand (left) on the mat. As you are coming to the handstand position, you put the other hand (right) down and shift your weight to it picking up the first hand (left). As your weight gets onto the second (right) hand, you bend at the waist sharply and split the legs bringing the kickup leg (right) down close to the corresponding hand (right). Next, stand up as you put the other foot (left) down. Practice this until you can do it with ease and with a fairly even 1, 2, 3, 4 rhythm.

3. Step 2 can now be modified by putting the hands down on a diagonal line with the hands turned 45° in the direction of the forward or takeoff foot (left). This puts the first hand (left) at the same place on the mat as in the Step 2 exercise but turned 45° in the corresponding direction (left). The second hand (right) is placed about 18 inches forward beyond where it was placed in the Step 2 exercise and is also turned 45° in the same direction as the other hand (left). The comedown onto one foot and then the other will leave you facing a little farther around than the hands in the same direction (left). This exercise requires a little more forceful kickup than the previous one and the pattern formed by the placement of the hands and the feet is about semicircular.

4. Now the groundwork is laid and the cartwheel itself can be done by simply turning the hands 90° instead of 45° and setting them down on the straight line in front of the forward (left) foot instead of the diagonal as in the previous exercise. Considerably more kickup force is needed to carry the balance through. The legs remain in the spread position and the feet come down on the same straight line as the hands. Recheck the description of action for the Cartwheel for full details.

CORRECTION OF ERRORS

A. Many beginners think of the cartwheel as a turning-over trick and, therefore, try to make a landing after the hand support by going over the top like a handspring. You can absorb the idea that the comedown is really a return trip from the kickup but facing a different direction by going through the four progressive learning steps described above.

B. Many cartwheel errors occur because there are angles where there should be straight lines. Keeping the shoulders back so that during the handstand part there is a straight line between the arms and the trunk will make for better support and a smoother sequence of movements. Getting the full leg swing up so that the body gets to be straight but not arched at the waist will add to the style and effectiveness of the cartwheel. Keeping the knees straight during the entire action will add force and form to your attempt.

C. A sluggish finish that does not result in an easy stand-up may be the result of failure to ride the weight over the far hand and even beyond before starting the bending at the waist, which brings the landing foot down. It is also necessary to make the comedown bend forceful and complete with straight knee in order for it to be most effective.

D. Putting the hands down off to the side of the straight line in front of the forward foot is an error that many find easy to commit. Putting the hands down more or less at the same time instead of quite separately and picking them up similarly is a common fault among those who consider themselves too weak to support themselves briefly on one arm at a time. Practice on the moving handbalance (Stunt No. 3) will help gain confidence to correct this error.

VARIATIONS AND COMBINATIONS

6.1. Running Cartwheel. To do a cartwheel from a preceding running start requires the learning of the hop-step technique to make possible a smooth transition from run to cartwheel. The last running step preceding the hop-step is onto the foot used for the kickup behind on the cartwheel (right, for example). While you are riding on this foot (right) at the end of the last running step, the other leg (left) is swung forward in a kind of kicking action and the arms are swung forward overhead. This forward kick is accompanied by a low forward hop from which the landing is on the same foot (right) again with the other leg (left) forward. The landing from the hop is with a bending knee and a forward lean so that the forward step follows immediately. This forward step is onto a bent leg (left) and is accompanied by the bending of the body forward to place the first hand for the cartwheel. The kickup of the back leg (right) as the hand reaches the mat gets the cartwheel rolling.

You may find this action easier to learn by following a progression beginning with the cartwheel from the one-step approach as described under description of action for Stunt No. 5. After reviewing this stunt, add the forward hop as you raise the leg forward and before stepping forward onto it. Next, learn to precede the hop with a forward swing of the forward-stepping leg and the arms. Next, try preceding the swing of arms and leg with a step onto the hopping foot. Now, learn to use several walking steps leading up to the last step, swing, hop-step, and cartwheel. When the walking approach is learned, the run can easily be substituted to complete the learning sequence.

A few admonitions here may help you to learn this important skill correctly so that it may be more useful in other running stunts. Do not lean back or even stand up straight as you take the arm and leg swing and hop. Keep a forward lean and a forward bend and use a long low type of hop. Do not land from the hop with a straight-knee, bouncy sort of landing but, instead, sink as you land, stepping forward immediately to the other foot.

6.2. Sideward Cartwheel.   From a standing position with the arms over-head and apart and the legs spread 20 to 30 inches apart, bend sideward forcefully (to the left, for example) lifting the opposite foot (right) laterally. Place the hand (left) on the mat beside the foot (left) and jump from that leg, riding on the hand (left) with the legs spread. Place the other hand (right) on the mat beside, but at a distance of 20 to 30 inches from, the first hand (left). Ride over onto the second hand (right) picking up the first (left). Bend sideward at the waist to bring the first foot (right) down beside the hand (right). Come to a stand facing the same direction and in the same position as at the start.

This type of cartwheel requires more flexibility and is harder to learn than the forward-bending type described previously. It has a certain beauty of its own and, in some circumstances, is more useful than the other type. It can be learned readily by those sufficiently flexible after learning the more ordinary kind first.

6.3. Series of Cartwheels.   To be able to do one cartwheel right after another, to give the appearance of a rolling wheel, it is necessary to have the single cartwheel under good control and in a straight line. The series can be done with either the regular (Stunt No. 6) or the sideward (Stunt No. 6.2) cartwheel, but the sideward cartwheel lends itself more readily to continuity than does the forward-bending type. In either case, you must acquire the skill of coming up to a momentarily balanced stand on the landing leg so that the placing of the second foot can also be the step that initiates the next cartwheel. If the forward bending cartwheel is used, there must also be a stronger than usual pivot or spin on the landing foot in order to turn 180° around to face into the next cartwheel. The arms swing through the stretched overhead position between cartwheels.

6.4. Reverse Cartwheel.   A cartwheel that is a regular cartwheel for one may be a reverse cartwheel for another. If you ordinarily kick up your right leg and go first onto your left hand for your cartwheel, you do a reverse cartwheel by kicking up your left leg and placing your right hand on the mat first. The ability to do a good cartwheel on your weak or awkward side is a worthwhile skill. It can be acquired most easily soon after you first learn to do the one-way cartwheel with facility.

6.5. One-Arm Cartwheels. Using the first or near arm exclusively for support during the cartwheel is somewhat easier than placing only the second or far hand on the mat for the stunt (Fig. 6.5). The near-arm cartwheels are easier on the kickup as they are almost the same as the ordinary two-arm cartwheel in the early stage. The comedown is more difficult since it must be executed without a shift of balance and from the unaccustomed hand. The far-arm cartwheel is more difficult on the kickup and more like the two-hand version on the comedown. Practice on moving handbalance (Stunt No. 4.3), hand-walking (Stunt No. 4.4), and reverse cartwheels (Stunt No. 6.4) will help you acquire the facility and control needed for the one-arm cartwheels.

Fig. 6.5. One-arm cartwheel.

6.6. Cartwheel to Handstand. Kick up with considerably less force than for a cartwheel, and place the hands farther apart on the floor to help stop the momentum. Special care should be taken to place the near hand in line with the front foot and to kick up straight behind in order to be vertical when the second hand comes to the floor. The movement stops when the far hand lands and the performer utilizes the technique previously described (see Stunt No. 4.5) to maintain the handstand position. The legs may stay spread until the handstand is reached and then close, or they may

Fig. 6.6. Cartwheel to handstand.

close to a joined position right after the kickup as shown here (see Fig. 6.6).

Stunt No. 7—SNAP UP (KIP-UP, MAT KIP)

DESCRIPTION OF ACTION

Roll back to a position in which your shoulders and the back of your neck and head are against the mat, your body is bent at the waist with your straight legs extended above your face, with the feet pointing toward the mat a few feet behind the head. The hands should be on the mat, at points just beside and a little behind the shoulders with fingers pointing outward or semi-outward from the shoulders.

The first movement is a relatively slow one and consists of a rolling forward action that results in lowering the hips to a position closer to the mat and in straightening the roundness of the upper back somewhat, but does not result in any great amount of opening at the waist nor does it remove the hands, neck, and shoulders from contact with the mat (Fig. 7A). After this rolling action has moved a few degrees, the kip or snap action is executed. This consists of an explosively fast opening or unbending at the waist swinging the straight legs through a circular arc forward-upward and around toward the mat (Fig. 7B). This explosive opening is

Fig. 7. Snap Up (Mat Kip). A. During rolling movement before snap. B. Opening explosively forward upward. C. Just before sit-up action starts. D. Low squat landing.

accompanied by a sudden push against the mat with both hands. As the body unbending carries the feet over toward the mat and lifts the mid-section upward, the knees bend, the feet turn outward and spread 12 to 18 inches apart ready for landing (Fig. 7C). After the opening is complete and just before the feet land, there is a sudden bending forward again at the waist and reaching forward with the arms and head. Almost immediately after this break to a sit-up, your feet land and you find yourself in a deep squat position on your feet (Fig. 7D) from which position you can come to an erect standing finish.

This low, deep squat, flat-footed landing is a somewhat ungraceful but very efficient and economical landing. It will permit you to get to your feet and stay there when your snap up is still not fully perfected. As you get more proficient and stronger with your snap up action, you can land in a high squat and maybe even a layout landing as described later (Stunt 7.4).

STEPS IN LEARNING

1. The first procedure is to learn two practice drill positions. The first of these, which we will call position one, is the same as that described above for the beginning of the snap up except that the arms are to be extended on the mat alongside the body with the hands palm down on the mat but out from the body 1 foot or so on either side. The second, position two, is most easily attained by first lying flat on the back with the arms alongside as they were in position one, then lift the hips up bending the knees, walking the feet as far as possible back under the hips to a position 12 to 18 inches apart with the entire soles of the feet on the mat and with the feet turned outward. This leaves the hips high and your weight resting on your shoulders, arms, neck and head, and feet.

2. Next, you learn to open slowly from position one reaching the extended legs through a long sweeping arc upward, then forward, and finally, at the last moment, bending the knees and putting the feet to the mat under the raised hips in position two. The arms pressing against the mat serve as a resistance to make possible slow and controlled body movements from position one to position two.

3. Add now a slight forward rolling action from position one preceding the body-opening movements that lead to position two. This rolling action will cause the direction of opening to be more forward-upward and less vertical than in the preceding exercise. This in turn will make it harder to keep your body in slow control and, therefore, this exercise will be a somewhat faster movement than in Step 2 but still not explosive.

4. When Step 3 has been repeatedly practiced so that the correct positions are being attained habitually, then it is time to add the explosive force. The movements will be the same as in Step 3 except that after the slow action has carried a few degrees, the body-opening action, the leg swing-over, and the resulting upward hip-lift are done with as much sudden force as possible. This results in a lifting of the head, arms, and shoulders

off the mat a few inches. The feet land first, then the hands, then the shoulders, neck, and head. There is no sit-up attempt and the final position is again approximately position two.

5. To practice the "break" or sit-up action by itself before putting the whole stunt together, stand with the feet apart and turned outward as they will be in the final landing for the snap up. Put your hands up by your shoulders, push your hips way forward bending your knees somewhat as you do so. From this awkward standing position, which simulates the air position just before the sit up, make a sudden forward bending at the waist at the same time bending the legs to drop the hips down near the mat between the feet into a deep squat and thrust the arms forward so that the armpits are over the knee caps.

6. To put the whole stunt together now take position one but put the hands on the mat up by the shoulders where they get a push, roll forward slightly, then explosively open as in Step 4 to the hips forward or arched position and just before the feet land, make the sit-up break as you have practiced it in Step 5 to the final deep squat landing.

CORRECTIONS OF ERRORS

A. Having the knees bent instead of straight during the unbending action or bending them too soon for the landing takes much of the power out of this body action and results in difficulty or even failure in coming to a stand. Emphasize the long sweeping arc described by the feet in each of the preparatory exercises so that you will be able to use it correctly in the finished product.

B. Getting a good lift but ending up on the back instead of on the feet is often the result of kipping too straight up. There should be a rolling movement before the kip and the direction of reach-out with the feet should be toward the front wall of the room before coming back to the mat under the hips.

C. Failure to break at the waist and sit up before the feet land will make it much more difficult to land on the feet and avoid falling back again.

D. Going through the movements too slowly without sufficient push and punch will also result in failure even if the movements are otherwise correct. It takes a sudden all-out effort at just the right time to get good results.

VARIATIONS AND COMBINATIONS

7.1. No-Hands Snap Up. On this stunt, instead of placing the hands on the mat near the shoulders and using them for a push-off, the hands are placed on the front of the leg above the knee (Fig. 7.1) or are kept free up along the side of the legs. This requires a little more efficiency on the other force elements in the stunt, especially more explosiveness. Some assistance to replace the hand push can be given by pushing back against the mat with the head at the moment of explosive snap.

Fig. 7.1. "No-hands" snap up starting position.

Fig. 7.2. Rolling to shoulders for shoulder spring.

7.2. Shoulder Spring. From a stand, squat and reach forward placing your hands wider apart than your shoulders, a yard or so ahead of your feet. Straightening your knees as for the start of a forward roll but more slowly, place the back of the head on the mat at a point no farther forward than the line between your hands and roll slowly onto your shoulders (Fig. 7.2). As soon as your shoulders come in contact with the mat, and while continuing to roll slowly over, execute the snap up as you have learned it from the instructions for Stunt No. 7.

7.3. Series of Shoulder Springs. The shoulder springs (Stunt No. 7.2) can be done in consecutive series of two or more by remaining in the squat balance on the feet at the end of one shoulder spring while reaching forward for the hand placement to start the second. Though consecutive, each one is separate and it is important to reach well out and to avoid a too early or too forceful leg straightening at the beginning of each shoulder spring.

7.4. Snap Up to Layout Landing. In order to be able to land in an arched-back stand-up landing from a snap up or a shoulder spring, it is necessary to get a very forceful snap and push from the mat or to have a very limber back or a moderate amount of each. On the layout landing the knees may be bent, although the straight-knee form is preferable, but the hips may not be bent at all (Fig. 8.4). The hyperextended or arched-body position at the time the feet come to the mat is essential, and there must be enough momentum to prevent falling backward so that you can come to a normal standing position soon after landing. The learning process is made easier by the temporary use of a rolled mat (Fig. 8E) from which to do the snap up or shoulder spring. This added height will make it possible for you to do the layout landing, especially if some assistance is given by a partner who will lift a little under the hips or middle of the back.

7.5. Snap Up with Half Twist. Starting from either the on-the-back position as for a snap up or from the shoulder spring beginning as described in Stunt No. 7.2, the twist is begun as the body is being straightened from the piked position. The twist is accomplished by the vigorous turning of the hips and legs to the left or right continuing until the feet land on the mat facing directly opposite to the direction they would face on a straight snap up. The upper body, shoulders, and head follow the lead of the hips in twisting around. Instead of a stand-up landing, which requires a very strong snap and arm push, a front support landing (as if ready for a push-up) can be the terminal position. In either form this makes a useful skill for part of a Floor Exercise routine.

Stunt No. 8—HEADSPRING

DESCRIPTION OF ACTION

From a standing start bend both knees deeply placing the hands on the mat a yard or so forward of the feet a little farther apart than shoulder width, with fingers pointing forward-outward (Fig. 8A). Without hesitation, straighten the legs while placing the fore part of the top of the head on the mat directly between the hands. As the knees straighten, the feet lose contact with the mat but remain fairly low with the legs about parallel to the mat as the weight is taken onto the head and hands. This jackknife headstand position is held while the performer shifts the balance over and past the point of support, taking pains to keep the top of the head (not the back part) in contact with the mat (Fig. 8B). When the angle between the mat and the performer's back (head to hips) has reached about a 45° angle, the vigorous unbending of the body at the waist and the strong push of the hands (as in Stunt No. 7, the snap up) lift the head off the mat and swing the feet over toward their landing on the mat (Fig. 8C). The rest of the action including the squat landing (Fig. 8D) is identical to that described for the snap up (Stunt No. 7). Having the knees straight from the time they leave the mat, through the brief jackknife headstand position, through the opening or kip action until just before landing is very important to both the appearance and the efficiency of the movements.

A

B

C

D

Fig. 8. Headspring. A. Leaning squat-reach start. B. Jackknife headstand overbalance just before kip. C. Forceful straightening and pushing. D. Squat landing.

STEPS IN LEARNING

1. It is not necessary to be able to accomplish the snap up (Stunt No. 7) before learning the headspring, but it is almost essential that the steps for learning the snap up should be followed and practiced as a preliminary to attempting the headspring.

2. An additional preparation recommended is the jackknife headstand, fallover. This starts by getting down on the hands and knees and placing the head and hands on the mat with the hands a little wider than the shoulders and the fore part of the head in contact with the mat directly between the hands. Next, the knees are straightened, putting the support on the toes, hands, and head. Now, while walking the feet up as far as possible without rolling past the *top*-of-the-head-to-the mat position, the bend at the waist is increased. Then, with a little push from the feet and push with the hands, the weight is taken entirely onto the head and hands. Holding this body-bent, knees-straight position and without losing the top-of-head-to-mat contact, the balance is forced over by the continuing hand push until the performer falls onto his back with a bump. As he lands, his head should still be back as if looking back where he came from. This exercise is designed to teach the straight-knee jackknife position and especially the top-of-the-head-to-mat contact held in spite of the constantly shifting balance.

3. The third step will be a partner-assisted attempt at the headspring itself with the head and hands placed on a raised area. First roll, or rather

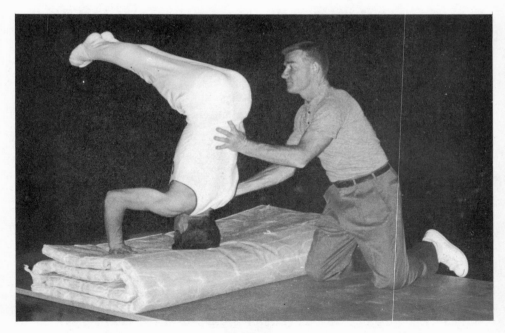

Fig. 8E. Using a folded mat "platform" for learning the headspring.

fold a smallish mat (say 5 feet x 10 feet) into about a four-thickness fold making a "platform" about 5 feet x 2 feet x 1 foot. Now, squat 1 foot or so away from the folded mat (facing the 2-foot width) place the hands and head (forehead) in a straight line in about the center of the folded mat. The assistant should kneel on the far side of the mat with his near hand on the performer's upper arm and the far hand ready to support under the back. The performer straightens his knees with enough force to shift his balance to his head and hands in the jackknife position and rides through the balance point to the 45° overbalance position without losing the top-of-the-head-to-mat contact before executing the kip action (Fig. 8E). The assistant lifts and controls during the kip action helping the performer to land on his feet in the squat landing. Both parties should take care that the performer's flying arms do not hit the spotter.

4. Soon the assistance of a spotter should become unnecessary and the performer can develop his rolled-mat headspring to the form described for the headspring. He will need to learn to place the hands and head on the mat *as* he straightens his knees instead of beforehand and he will learn to spring with a little more force in order to move through the head- and hand-supported jackknife position more quickly so that the motion is continuous from the stand through the squat, the spring, the kip, and the landing.

5. The final step, of course, is to remove the folded mat platform and do the headspring on the flat mat. There may be a tendency at first to spring too forcefully from the legs and, thus, overturn the balance before there is time to kip. It would be well, at first, to move through the headstand a little more slowly than normal to avoid this.

CORRECTION OF ERRORS

A. The most characteristic mistake to cause an inferior performance of the headspring is the failure to ride through solidly on the top of the head. If the chin is allowed to move toward the chest, the performer starts rolling to the back of the head and the neck no longer supports the weight well. Care should be taken in every stage of learning that the head maintains its vertical position while the body rotates on over to a 45° angle past the vertical.

B. A second common error is the failure to overbalance far enough in the piked position before starting the opening movement. Practicing Step 2 in the learning series above will help. It would also be helpful to have an observer tell the performer when he has reached the correct angle and for him to wait until he gets the call to execute his kip action.

C. It is also not uncommon for the performer to attempt to spring himself over to his feet with a too strong leg drive instead of taking just enough drive to move through the jackknife headstand to overbalance, and then use the explosive force of the body straightening to effect the rotation onto the feet. Using a learning position that emphasizes the jackknife headstand position held and then overbalanced should eliminate this error.

D. The other errors are those that are common also to the snap up and have been covered under the Correction of Errors section for that stunt. Reference back to that material should prove helpful in detecting and eliminating errors in the headspring.

VARIATIONS AND COMBINATIONS

8.1. Series of Headsprings.   To proceed from one headspring to the next in a consecutive series necessitates staying in the squat position after landing, and then reaching well forward to place the hands and head a yard or so in front of the feet while straightening the legs into the jackknife position.   The final headspring of a series of three or four could be done with the layout landing (see Stunt No. 8.4) to beautify the series.

8.2. Headspring from Headstand.   After a straight body headbalance, the headspring technique may be used to regain a standing position by bending sharply at the waist while at the same time moving the hands from the tripod position to the straight-line pattern and overbalancing.   When overbalanced about 45° past the vertical, the performer executes the kiplike ·headspring action to bring himself over to his feet. A similar technique can be used to move from a handbalance to a jackknife headstand and immediately into the second half of the headspring action.

8.3. Headspring with Half Twist.   The regular headspring start (or the headstand or handstand starts as in Stunt No. 8B above) can precede a hip-twisting kip action similar to that described in Stunt No. 7.5 to the front-support landing or even to the stand-up landing on the feet.   This stunt is particularly adaptable to Floor Exercise work.

8.4. Headspring to Layout Landing.   Somewhat easier, but essentially similar to the snap up to layout landing (Stunt No. 7.4) is the headspring to layout landing.   As in Stunt No. 7.4, the essential item is the arched or hyperextended hip position on the final landing (Fig. 8.4).   The knees may

Fig. 8.4.   Layout   landing   from headspring.

be slightly bent, the landing should be on the balls of the feet. A strong kip action and a strong push with the arms are needed. A flexible back is of great advantage in learning to accomplish this landing readily. Doing the headspring from the folded mat platform can be of considerable help in first learning the layout landing as also can effective hand-spotting by an assistant (Fig. 8E).

Stunt No. 9—FORWARD HANDSPRING

DESCRIPTION OF ACTION

After a few running steps the tumbler does a forward-traveling low hop on his "kickup" foot accompanied by a forward-upward swinging of both arms and a forward swing of the "takeoff" foot so that during the hop the takeoff foot is well ahead of the hopping foot (Fig. 9A). The landing on the hopping foot is followed immediately by the landing of the other foot 24 inches or so forward of it and by the forward bending of the waist to place the hands on the mat another 2 or 3 feet forward of the front foot. The hand placement is accompanied by a kick up behind with the back or kickup leg, with head up and straight arms as in the kickup to handstand (Stunt No. 4), but with great force (Fig. 9B). The kickup and the jump of the takeoff foot carry the body through the inverted handbalance and into an arched overbalanced position on the hands. The hands are then picked up from the mat (Fig. 9C) and pulled in close to the body; the head position is changed from looking at the mat to a head-down, chin-on-chest position; and the body is bent and the legs are prepared for landing as in the snap up (Stunt No. 7) and the headspring (Stunt No. 8). The squat landing for the handspring (Fig. 9D) need not be so low as in the snap up and headspring because the added height and speed make a high squat landing more comfortable and more feasible.

STEPS IN LEARNING

1. A number of the previously described skills are necessary prerequisites to the safe and logical learning of the handspring. The standing kickup to momentary handstand (Stunt No. 4), the cartwheel (Stunt No. 6), and especially the running cartwheel (Stunt No. 6.1) are important leadup skills. The squat landing should be learned by at least attempting to learn the snap up (Stunt No. 7) and/or headspring (Stunt No. 8).

2. A preparatory exercise specifically for the handspring is a kickup to a handstand from a standing start, arching the back and bending the knees, turning the feet outward, falling on over through the handstand until the feet land on the mat without letting the arms bend and without picking up the hands or ducking the head down. After the feet land, the head may drop and the arms may bend. The final position is more or less on the back. It is important that the shoulders stay back in line between the

CARL A. RUDISILL LIBRARY
LENOIR RHYNE COLLEGE

A

B

C

D

Fig. 9. Forward Handspring. A. During the hop portion of the run-hop-step approach. B. Kickup toward handstand. C. During flight before sit-up action starts. D. Squat landing.

hands and hips during the handstand and the fall-over, and that the arms stay straight and the head stays up, looking at the mat. The first few of these fall-overs can be made more comfortable with the well-placed hand of an assistant under the middle of the back to slow down the descent.

3. The next step in learning the handspring involves two, or better, three people working together. Two spotters kneel facing each other 2 to 3 feet apart. The performer kicks to a handstand between them, bends his knees, falls overbalanced, and then, while being supported strongly by the spotters, picks up his hands, ducks his head, bends at the waist, and comes, thus assisted, to the squat landing. The spotters have their near hand on his upper arm and their far hands in the middle of the back. They move closer together as they support his weight. Performer and spotters should both be alert to the danger of flying arms coming into forceful contact with helpful faces. One spotter instead of two, though less protective, can suffice (Fig. 9E). A soft landing surface is recommended.

Fig. 9E. One-man spotting for forward handspring.

4. Stronger kickups, less spotting, and finally a running (with hop-step) approach should be succeeding stages in the learning process. The straight-arm and head-up handstand ride-over, however, remains the basis for a good handspring performance, even with the increased speed and force.

CORRECTION OF ERRORS

A. Bent arms and early ducking of the head are the most common errors and are best corrected by extra practice on the rather slow-motion handspring with strong spotting.

B. Shoulders forward is another common mistake. A correction may be made by placing the hands farther forward at the start without, at the same time, putting the shoulders farther forward. Also helpful will be the practice of a wall-supported handstand with the shoulders farther from the wall than the hands or hips.

C. A third common error in the forward handspring is the failure to open up all the way to an arched handstand with the feet reaching over toward the landing before bending at the waist for a sit-up landing. This results in an incomplete kickup, a too early break at the waist and usually an underturned finish on the seat instead of the feet. Practice on the handstand arch-over (Step 2) and on the partner-supported handspring (Step 3) should remedy this error.

VARIATIONS AND COMBINATIONS

9.1. Handspring to Layout Landing. This variation is similar to the layout landing from the headspring (Stunt No. 8.4). This landing applied to the handspring results in a more difficult, but much superior handspring. The run, hop-step approach should be brisk and smooth with continuing forward momentum. The hand placement should be well forward of the front foot and with locked elbows and head up. An extension action in the shoulder girdle can give the tumbler a bounce-off lift from the hands at this stage of the handspring resulting in a higher arc and making the layout landing easier and the handspring more spectacular (Fig. 9.1).

Fig. 9.1. Layout landing from handspring.

9.2. Handspring to Stepout Landing.   The technique is exactly the same as for Stunt No. 9.1 except for the landing action which is a one-foot-ahead step-out action (Fig. 9.2) instead of a two-feet-at-a-time landing. The body

Fig. 9.2. Stepout landing from handspring.

position is still a hips-forward layout, but the feet land separately and one ahead of the other by a distance of from 1 to 3 feet. The step-out landings are useful when it is desired to follow a handspring with another stunt for which the proper takeoff is from one foot, as for example, a cartwheel (Stunt No. 6), another handspring, or a roundoff (Stunt No. 10). There is a slightly different variety of handspring to a stepout which is used when the object is to maintain maximum speed out of the handspring into the next stunt. This continuous speed variety of handspring walkout contains a forward bend at the waist during the flight interval between the liftoff of the hands and the step-step landing of the feet, instead of the maintenance of the layout, forward-hip position.

9.3. Tinsica.   The stunt commonly called a tinsica is essentially a handspring to walkout with the hands being placed one at a time, and one a foot or more forward of the other instead of simultaneously and side by side. The hand placed second and farther forward corresponds to the first landing foot. The most ordinary sequence then would be left hand, right hand,

Fig. 9.3.   Tinsica.

right foot, left foot.   As compared to the handspring walkout, it has a little less shoulder bounce and a little more rolling continuity (Fig. 9.3).

The authentic Arabian tinsica is somewhat different.   Instead of being straight ahead, the body is turned 20° or so to the right or left while rotating.   The direction of this turn corresponds to the back or kickup leg.   In other words, it is a little toward a cartwheel from a handspring.   The hand placement, especially the far hand or second hand to be placed, is also somewhat sideways as in a cartwheel.   The landing on one foot (say the right) is with the foot turned outward to about right angle to the direction of motion and with the knee bent.   The back is arched as in the handspring to step-out landing, rather than bent as in the cartwheel.   The head is looking back over the shoulder (right) toward the hand (right) coming up off the mat.   The other foot comes down soon after the first in a stepping forward action.

9.4. Two-Feet Takeoff Forward Handspring.   From a brisk run, take a fairly long but low hurdle (jump from one foot to two) landing on the balls of the feet with the hands over the head and with a slight forward body-bend (Fig. 9.4A).   Bounce immediately from the feet, bending forward more at the waist at the same time to bring the hands down to the mat.   The landing on the hands is an overturned, slightly piked, handstand position with arms straight and head up looking at the mat in front of the hands (Fig. 9.4B).   Bounce immediately off the hands with a body action similar to the second part of a headspring, landing on the feet in either a squat or layout landing.

9.5. Walk-Overs and Front Limbers.   Tumblers with very flexible backs often learn forward limbers or walk-overs, which are really forward handsprings to layout landings or step-out landings without the *spring*.   The

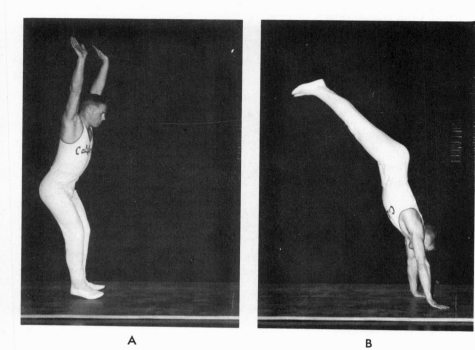

A   B

Fig. 9.4. Two-feet takeoff forward handspring. A. Just before takeoff. B. Landing on hands in slight pike.

A   B

Fig. 9.5. **Limbers.** A. Two-feet limber. B. Walkover.

starting actions are the same as handsprings, except that the run and hop-step are unnecessary. A standing start is satisfactory. The straight-arm, head-up, kickup through the handstand need not be as forceful as for handsprings, and the hands, arms, and head maintain their positions until the feet or foot lands and accepts the body weight. Only then are the hands lifted from the mat or floor. The full and complete body arch (hyper-extension) is essential to the performance of these stunts. When the landing is on both feet, these are usually called front or forward limbers (Fig. 9.5A). When the landing is on one foot with a step-out to the other, they are called walk-overs (Fig. 9.5B). In the walk-overs, the legs usually maintain their kickup split all the way to the landing.

9.6. Series of Forward Handsprings.   In order to do several forward hand-springs in a consecutive series, you must either use the step-out form (Stunt 9B) so that each handspring can start with a one-foot kickup or use the two-foot takeoff style (Stunt No. 9D) for the second and following handsprings. Of these two choices, the first is by far the more frequently used and the easier to maintain momentum.   The step-out handspring is modified slightly as indicated in the description of the stunt to facilitate the getting into the beginning of the next one with maximum continuity. This modification consists of bending forward at the waist before landing in the step-out, and a leaning and reaching forward for the next hands' placement so that as soon as the feet land there can be an immediate kickup of the back foot for the next handspring. Tinsicas, Arabian tinsicas, and walk-overs also lend themselves well to use in consecutive series.

Stunt No. 10—ROUNDOFF

DESCRIPTION OF ACTION

The roundoff is an apparently fairly simple, although actually very diffi-cult, but important fundamental tumbling skill. Roughly, it is a kind of running cartwheel with a two-foot landing facing opposite to the direction of run, and is used for the purpose of converting a forward run into a back-ward facing takeoff position for backward rotating handsprings and somer-saults. The correct performance technique varies considerably between the slow or short approach type, and the fast or long approach type.

In either case, the run and hop-step, as previously described for the run-ning cartwheel (Stunt No. 6.1) and running handspring (Stunt No. 9), pre-cede the roundoff. The hand placement, as the body is bent forward and the kickup of the back leg starts, is (for the fast approach type) in the same sequence and pattern as for the cartwheel (Fig. 10A). The hands are placed quite separately in both time and space with the hand corresponding to the forward foot (we shall say left) coming to the mat first about a yard forward of the foot and with the fingers pointing at right angle to the direction of

A   B

C   D

Fig. 10. Roundoff.   A. After the run-hop-step approach, the cartwheel-like start.   B. Just past midway the legs are moving side by side.   C. The sharp bend and push away.   D. The overturned stand-up finish.

run (to the left in this case). As the kickup puts the body weight on this left arm and moving forward, the body turns gradually from its original forward facing position to a sideward facing position. As the second (right) hand comes to the mat facing parallel to the first and about 18 inches beyond it in the same straight line, it is driven to the mat with a particularly strong force (Fig. 10B). Coincidental with and after the second hand drive come the pickup of the first hand and the beginning of the snap down. The snap down consists of a sharp bend at the waist with straight legs, and the push away from the mat with the second (right) hand (Fig. 10C). The landing on the two feet is in a fairly erect stand-up position (Fig. 10D). The second 90° of turn takes place during this snap down. Soon after the initial kickup, the takeoff leg catches up to the kickup leg and stays beside it (a few inches apart) so that the legs move in unison during the rest of the roundoff (Fig. 10B). At the landing then, the feet are several inches apart, facing the direcion from which the run started. The knees may bend considerably at the last moment before the landing, and the feet land nearly flat if the succeeding trick is to be a backward handspring (Fig. 10D), or they may stay almost straight and the landing be high on the balls of the feet if the succeeding trick is to be a high backward somersault.

If the run is short or slow or both, a somewhat different technique is required to get the 180° turn and a strong snap down. The short-run technique calls for the placement of the second hand (right) on a spot closer to the first hand and to the side of the straight line and with the fingers pointing almost back in the direction from which the approach started. In other words, more of the 180° turn is done before the second hand is placed, and the snap down is done from a handstand that is facing more nearly backward before the snap down starts.

STEPS IN LEARNING

1. The cartwheel (Stunt No. 6) is a most helpful preparation for the round-off. The run, hop-step approach as used for the cartwheel should also be well learned.
2. Modify a standing cartwheel by delaying the lead leg after the kickup until the other leg (takeoff leg) can catch up with it, closing the split within a few inches, then riding over onto the far hand, bend sharply at the waist (but not the knees) bringing both feet to the mat for a simultaneous landing about 6 inches apart.
3. Add more speed to the kickup and snap down so that by pushing away with the far hand, the hand will leave the mat before the feet land.
4. Next, add the run, hop-step approach increasing the speed on successive tries and reaching a bit farther out for the hand placement.

CORRECTION OF ERRORS

A. Weak roundoffs are most often caused by failure to keep the knees straight enough during the middle and latter part of the action.

B. Twisted roundoffs, where the performer lands with his upper body still twisted or with one shoulder low, are often the result of too strong a push with the first hand and too weak a push with the second. The emphasis should be on the slam-down drive of the second hand at the time of the beginning of the snap down.

C. Crooked roundoffs, where the tumbler lands way off mat center, may be the result of any of a variety of causes. The cause may be the failure to put the hands down separately on a line with the front foot and parallel to the length of the mat. Crookedness may be the result of putting the hands down too close to the front foot. There should be a fairly long reach especially with a fast run. A third prevalent cause is using a full-speed approach and then attempting to turn both the shoulders and the hands around past the 90° turn too early and too far, as if doing a limited approach roundoff.

VARIATIONS AND COMBINATIONS

There have been several variations indicated in the above description. The difference between the limited approach and full-speed approach roundoffs has been described. The differences between the whole-footed knee-bent landing leading to a backward handspring or a backward roll, and the ball-of-the-foot straight-knee bounce landing leading to a high lift as for a swan jump or backward somersault have also been delineated. Combinations involving roundoffs will be described later in connection with the description of the stunt that is combined with the roundoff (for example, backward somersaults).

4

Some More Advanced Basic Tumbling Skills

Stunt No. 11—FORWARD SOMERSAULT (Downswing)

DESCRIPTION OF ACTION

Run forward with moderate speed and execute a long, low hurdle (jump from one foot to two) with the legs hanging at full length from the hips and the feet barely clearing the mat. During the hurdle flight, the arms are both lifted to an overhead reach with slightly bent elbows. The landing from the hurdle is in a slightly bent, forward-at-the-waist position, with the arms up as just indicated, the eyes looking forward-downward at the mat several feet ahead, with the weight on the balls of the feet and the knees nearly straight (Fig. 11A).

The takeoff is a bounce off the balls of the feet accomplished by ankle extension and knee straightening. With the bounce there is an accompanying forward bending at the waist, forward-downward swinging of the arms, and ducking of the head (Fig. 11B). After the feet leave the mat, the knees are bent, the hands come to grasping positions on the shins, and the arms bend pulling the knees to the chest and the feet to the buttocks (Fig. 11C). This tuck position is held briefly and then released. The body and knees straighten to a stand-up landing (Fig. 11D). Thus is accomplished a complete forward circle in the air.

STEPS IN LEARNING

1. The tucked forward roll, the running dive-roll and the forward handspring should be learned before attempting the forward somersault. Forward somersaults off the springboard into the water and on the trampoline are excellent preparations for the somersault on the mats.

2. Prepare a platform of mats 1 foot or more in thickness and at least 30 inches wide and 5 feet long. This can be done fairly satisfactorily by folding a 5 foot x 10 foot mat into three thicknesses and putting a second and

Fig. 11. Forward Somersault.   A. At the point of takeoff.   B. Moving into the tuck.   C. Rotating in the tucked position.   D. Landing.

possibly a third similarly folded mat on top of it (Fig. 11E). From a standing (without run) takeoff position similar to the takeoff position described above for the running somersault, lean forward slightly with legs straight and weight high on toes, then with a very quick bounce-type bending and straightening of legs, spring into a high dive roll onto the platform of mats, finishing with a tight, wide (knees apart for safety) tuck. When this can be done with consistency and a minimum of forward travel, go on to the next steps.

3. From similar takeoff position as in Step 2 above, but with body bent forward more before the start and with a fairly small spring (to limit height), do a tucked roll onto the pile of mats without putting the hands on the mat (as in Step 2), but bringing the hands directly to the shins and rolling across the shoulders and back in the knees-apart tucked position. Repeat many times.

4. Combining the takeoff position, spring, and height of Step 2 with the immediate ducking and tucking of Step 3, the result should be a tucked spin in the air to a seat-and-feet tucked landing on the soft mat pile. Releasing the grasp on the shins just before landing and putting the hands down alongside the seat at the moment of contact will soften the blow and start developing the habit and timing-sense of opening for the landing which is such an important part of the finished product and so essential for safety. With or without an assist on the back of neck or shoulders by a spotter's quick hand, the performer should begin to spin enough that the feet are landing before the seat before going on to the next step.

5. The running approach should be added by easy stages. First, a forward jump from two feet to the arms-overhead ball-of-the-feet takeoff position should be substituted for the standing takeoff of Step 4. Next, a single step and low hurdle should precede the takeoff. After several successful single-step efforts, more steps, and later, faster steps, and eventually running steps should be incorporated into the approach. As the momentum increases with the more and more complete approach, several precautions must be taken. A tendency to be leaning too far forward at the takeoff results in a long forward travel that could overshoot the landing platform pile of mats. More height and spin obtained from the approach or portion thereof can result in overspinning unless stress is placed on *opening out* of the tuck. Underspin (with moderation) is a much safer error than overspin. If the landing is on very bent legs, they should be straightening by the time they hit, working out against the mat rather than waiting till the mat hits them. This will help protect the knees from the landing forces. Ideally, the landing should be in a standing-up position with only a slight knee bend to absorb the shock.

6. The thickness of the landing pile should be gradually reduced as the tumbler progresses in his control and demonstrates that he needs the protection less. Hand spotting by an experienced and alert spotter (Fig. 11F) can assist this transition toward the unassisted somersault onto the level surface.

Fig. 11E. Using the folded-mat pile for learning the forward somersault.

Fig. 11F. Helpful hand spotting for the forward somersault.

CORRECTION OF ERRORS

A. The downswing forward somersault is not meant to be a particularly high somersault, but is meant to turn over fast at about head or shoulder height. If the tumbler fails to achieve even this amount of height, it may well be that his legs are not springy enough, but it may, on the other hand, be caused by poor technique. Ball-of-the-foot takeoffs, quick knee and ankle action, and a forceful low hurdle are all essential to a good spring in this somersault. The two errors most likely to result in too little height are a premature forward bend and an excessive forward lean. The takeoff position should be standing tall with a very little hips-back, forward-bent position at that moment. It should also be a near vertical position with the center of mass nearly over (not way forward of) the feet. The forward momentum of the approach will move the flight of the somersault sufficiently forward for most purposes without adding a substantial forward body angle at the takeoff. The excessive forward-bending and forward-leaning errors can often be best corrected by somersaulting up onto a high, close mat pile.

B. Lack of sufficient spinning speed is the most common of errors. This usually is caused by a delayed or sluggish forward bend or by a loosely pulled tuck. Another possible cause is the bending of the knees before the takeoff-drive-through-straight-legs has fully contributed to the rotational force. This can also cause lack of height. Repetitious practice with these possible causes checked and corrected one by one are necessary. Using a solid or springy takeoff board and a mat pile for added facility and comfort will be helpful in these practices. Explosiveness is an essential feature of this somersault.

VARIATIONS AND COMBINATIONS

11.1. Forward Somersault from a Forward Handspring. The forward handspring portion should be an especially forceful, somewhat overturned handspring from a good run to a layout landing on the ball of the feet with arms overhead (Fig. 11.1A). Doing a superior forward handspring by using the head-up, arms-straight, shoulder-girdle-bounce features as described in Stunt No. 9 and No. 9.1 is very important to the success of a handspring and forward somersault combination. The bounce from the handspring landing into the air for the somersault should be from almost straight knees and from the ball of the feet. There is not time to wait for balance or orientation, visual or kinesthetic. The balance must be a little forward so that the takeoff can be immediate albeit somewhat blind. With the takeoff comes the immediate bending of the body, ducking of the head, and, very quickly, the tuck (Fig. 11.1B). The landing may be either on two feet or with a step-out depending upon what is to follow.

11.2. Forward Somersault Series (Bounding Forward Somersaults). In order to do a second downswing forward somersault, and possibly a third or

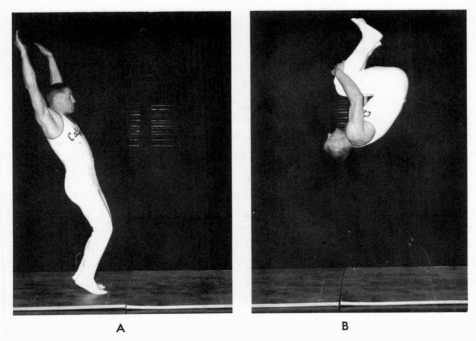

A   B

Fig. 11.1. Forward somersault from forward handspring. A. The landing of the handspring just before somersault takeoff. B. The tucked somersault.

fourth in immediate succession, it is helpful to do each one excellently, overturning each somersault slightly, landing with a slight forward lean on the balls of the feet in a stand-up position with the arms overhead (as in Fig. 11.1A). The succeeding somersault is then started with a quick bounce from this takeoff position. In order to maintain forward momentum, which helps each takeoff, the somersaults should be done with as much forward travel as is feasible without sacrificing the modest height that is necessary to complete and slightly overturn each somersault. A higher than usual somersault is to be avoided. This combination is an *advanced* technique done well by only the very best tumblers.

11.3. The Upswing Forward Somersault. This type of forward somersault in comparison to the downswing forward somersault (Stunt No. 11) is usually done with a faster and longer running approach. During the long, low hurdle the arms are both moved downward and backward and held in a slightly bent position in preparation for an upswing movement that accompanies and follows the landing on two feet at the end of the hurdle and the takeoff into the somersault. The position of the feet on the mats on this contact is less up on the toes than it is for the downswing forward somersault. It is more of a ball-and-heel landing followed very soon by the heel-ball takeoff. The feet are on the mat a little longer than on a toe-bounce takeoff. The forward upward swing of the slightly bent arms, which accompanies the takeoff, only continues to about the point where the hands are head-height, then the hands are returned quickly to the shin-grasping tucked position. The brisk forward-upward swing of the arms is accompanied by an equally brisk forward bending of the head and trunk to start the forward rotation of the body. This ducking and bending cannot wait until the arms are ready to cut down after their lift, without seriously slowing down the rotation. Excellent height and far superior turn-over can be attained by this early start into the spin. After a brief, but tight, tuck, the hands release the shins, and the legs and body straighten out to a stand-up landing.

11.4. Forward Somersault to a Step-out. The upswing forward somersault is the best type from which to step-out into a roundoff, or a forward handspring. The downswing somersault also is often used in this manner, especially when it has followed a previous handspring or somersault. The step-out consists of coming out of the tuck with one foot forward of the other (Fig. 11.4) and landing with a natural running-step action with slightly bent

Fig. 11.4. The beginning of the leg separation for a step-out landing from a forward somersault.

knees and with arms forward-upward. The body balance as the step is taken should be forward so that there is no delay moving into the next stunt. The somersault, therefore, should be overturned, and the tuck should be held even longer than for the two-feet landing.

Fig. 11.5. Back-swing lift (Russian) for the forward somersault.

11.5. Backswing Forward Somersault (Russian Front). For a powerful lift from a short run as is so important in Floor Exercise, the backswing is very useful. The run and takeoff are those described for the backswing dive and roll (Stunt No. 5.2). Soon after the takeoff, the knees start to bend and the body starts to bend to start the forward rotation (Fig. 11.5). The head is soon ducked and the hands grasp the shins in a tight tuck position. Opening from the tuck and coming into the landing are the same as for other forward somersaults.

Stunt No. 12—BACKWARD HANDSPRING (Flip-Flop, Flip-Flap)

DESCRIPTION OF ACTION

From an erect standing position with arms down at the sides, the first action is a backward movement of the extended arms toward the full backward extension prior to the forward swing. This backward movement of the arms is accompanied by a slight backward lean of the body, losing the balance slowly backward. As the arms are reaching the back end of their swing, the knees start to bend. The forward swing of the arms then accompanies the knee-bending so that the knees reach the depth of their bend (which is at right angle or deeper) as the arms are passing the vertical posi-

A

B

C

D

Fig. 12. Backward Handspring. A. At lowest part of sit start, arms swinging forward. B. The strong swing of arms and spring of legs puts hyperextended body in midair. C. The landing on the hands with straight knees. D. The snap down and push away with knees still straight.

tion on their way forward (Fig. 12A). The continuing forceful forward swing of the arms is accompanied by the equally forceful straightening of the legs and the forward-upward movement of the hips. The arms continue their free, loose, extended swing to the farthest overhead backward extended position that they can attain. This is accompanied by the continuing extension of the legs, backward throw of the head, and hyperextension (arch) of the back. The combination of these actions results in the feet leaving the ground and the body being airborne in an extended, arched position rotating backward (Fig. 12B). This rotation is relatively low and fast and the time in the air is very brief.

The landing is on the hands with the arms slightly bent and the hands, head, body, and legs in a position as for a handstand, but with the body fully arched (Fig. 12C). This complete arch includes the continued pull of the arms as far as possible backward bringing the shoulders in line with the curve extending from the heels to the hands.

Immediately following the landing on the hands, but not preceding it, the body is bent sharply at the waist, the arms extend, and the hands push away from the mat (Fig. 12D). This action is similar to the handstand jerk (see Stunt No. 4.1) but starts from the straight-knee (or almost straight) handstand-landing position (Fig. 12C) instead of the bent-knee handstand and moves faster because of the momentum from the first half of the back handspring. The landing on both feet in a stand-up position is usually done with a slight knee bend to soften it, but varies according to what movement is to follow the backward handspring.

STEPS IN LEARNING

1. In general, a considerable facility with more elementary tumbling stunts such as rolls, headsprings, and handsprings would be a helpful background for learning the backward handspring. Specifically, the momentary handstand and handstand jerk are almost necessary preliminaries to effective learning of this stunt.

2. To practice and learn the snap down portion or second half of the backward handspring, do a handstand with the hands 18 inches to 2 feet away from the wall with the feet (knees straight) resting against the wall. Without bending the knees, increase the arch in the back by moving the shoulders farther away from the wall, keeping the feet against the wall and slightly bending the arms. This, then, simulates the landing-on-the-hands position in the middle of the backward handspring. As the shoulders continue to move farther from the wall, the feet will leave the wall. At this point, bend forcefully and completely at the waist and push away with the hands by straightening the arms. The knees stay straight during this snap down, but bend some just before the feet land on the mat.

3. The spotter-supported backward bend from standing to handstand with snap down is the next learning step. Two spotters face each other in a

Fig. 12E. Layback over the shoulder carryover spotting for learning the backward handspring.

kneeling position beside (one on each side) and a little behind the performer, both placing their near hands on his knee and their far hands on the small of his back. As the performer, with arms overhead and head way back, starts bending and leaning backward, the spotters bend their far arms turning their bodies toward the performer's back, and bringing their shoulders against his back very near their own hands. As the performer bends backward over their shoulders reaching and looking for the mat, the spotters carry his weight on their hands and shoulders controlling his legs with their hands on his knees. (See Fig. 12E for demonstration by one spotter. Two are preferable when inexperienced.) As or before the performers hands reach the mat, the spotters, with both arms, lift the performer's lower body to help him acquire the arched handstand landing position. As the performer begins to carry his own weight on his arms, he should shift his shoulders on through into the same position as that which preceded the snap down in Step 2. The spotters, with sufficient but not excessive support, help him acquire this pre-snap down position and then, when his balance is moving on through the handstand, they should release him so that he can execute the straight-knee snap down with his own power.

4. While practicing and overlearning Step No. 3, the performer can alternately by practicing the first part of the backward handspring as an exercise by itself without attempting any turn-over action. For this exercise follow the "Description of Action" section above from the beginning including the backward lean, swing of the arms, and spring, but *not* including the for-

Fig. 12F. The starting position for one-man hand spotting of full-effort backward handspring.

Fig. 12G. The midway position for spotting backward handspring.

ward swing of the hips, backward throw of the head, or hyperextension of the back.

5. Now, with complete two-man spotting as in Step No. 3, the performer goes through Step 4 in slow motion continuing right into the back-bending over the spotters' shoulders action of Step 3, finishing as that exercise does with the straight-knee snap down. Little by little more speed and with it more spring can be added to the effort of the performer, requiring less support from the spotters. Full effort and full speed by the performer should result in minimum and then the absence of help from the spotters. (See Figs. 12F and 12G for one-man spotting of full speed effort.)

CORRECTION OF ERRORS

A. Failure to get a complete, free, and forceful arm swing will result in an insufficient or too slow backward rotation. Getting the arms from the hang directly into or near the backward extended or cocked position (Fig. 12A) before starting the backward-leaning sitting action will help prevent the hurried return that results from the incorrect action of putting the arms forward and starting the sit action while swinging the arms backward. The arms need time to get to the farthest possible backward point of their swing before the other actions require them to start forward. It is also important to keep a loose straightness to the arms during their swing so that the hands swing like rocks tied to the end of ropes. The arms on the return swing then must be swung through with maximum speed to the farthest point they will go, and held completely back over-head until the hands contact the mat and after. It is also important that as the hands land, they be at least shoulder width apart and point straight ahead or a little outward.

B. A too high or lobbing backward handspring is usually due to insufficient backward lean while cocking the arms and bending the legs prior to the forceful throwing action. It is, of course, quite possible to lean backward too much and, as a result, be too low in the flight. The stunt should be high enough that with good rotational speed the performer can land in the well-arched handstand with only slightly bent arms and not so high that he tends to drop down onto his hands or overturn beyond the over-hung handstand before making contact.

C. Although the forward bending of the trunk over the knees (while cocking the arms prior to the throw) to any pronounced degree is an error that will put the backward handspring in bad balance and delay the throw, the other extreme is also an error. The shoulders should not be kept behind or directly over the hips during the sit action, but should be allowed to move forward slightly in relation to the hips to permit a more complete arm preparation and a more forceful trunk movement following.

D. A "curl down" or "fold down" instead of a snap down results when knees are allowed to bend a great deal on the handstand landing and afterward. The result of this weak second half is that the feet come to the mat while the hands remain on or near the mat. No effective push-away and stand-up finish can be made with a severely bent knee action on this final phase. A little knee bend can result in a fairly good snap down. The straight-knee snap down (Fig. 12D) is by far the most effective kind for the backward handspring. The knees, of course, may and usually do bend just before the feet hit the mat, but the beneficial effect of the straight-knee action has already been applied before this point.

E. Another common error that must be mentioned is the tendency in the early stages of learning to start the body bend of the snap down before the hands land on the mat. This takes away most of the effectiveness of the snap down action. Practicing Step 2 and Step 3 above will help pre-vent or cure this error.

VARIATIONS AND COMBINATIONS

12.1. Backward Handspring Series. To proceed quickly, forcefully, and smoothly from one backward handspring to another requires excellent per-formance technique on each individual backward handspring. Each part is important in its contribution to the whole, but in the series the emphasis must be placed on the perfection and power in the second half or snap down part of each one. The snap down should be strong enough that when the feet land the body is already leaning backward into the next backward handspring. The snap down is strengthened by the forceful

Fig. 12.1. The landing position from one backward handspring in preparation for another.

bend at the waist, the keeping of the knees straight, and the push-away from the slightly bent-arm handstand by strongly straightening the arms and pushing down with the hands. The landing position between back handsprings should be bent-kneed, flat-footed, and backward leaning. The arms, immediately following their push-away, hesitate a moment extended more or less in the direction of the mat that they have just left until about the time the feet land. Then they swing freely and powerfully and straight back overhead (Fig. 12.1) toward the handstand landing of the next backward handspring. The legs maintain their bent position during the landing between back handsprings and for a brief transitional period (Fig. 12.1) while the feet stay on the mat and then drive, straightening to send the body into the next backward handspring. Learning a single backward handspring following immediately a handstand jerk (Stunt No. 4.1) is a helpful preliminary to learning a series. This exercise, as well as the series, will require spotting from one or more helpers either by hand (Fig. 12G), or with a safety belt with ropes held by two spotters (Fig. 13F).

12.2. Backward Handspring from Roundoff. This combination may well be learned before the series of backward handsprings, but the above information about the series should be well understood because it is applicable in most details to the roundoff backward handspring. It is important also to have acquired facility and control with the roundoff before adding the backward handspring to it. In the transition between the roundoff and the backward handspring, the straight-knee snap down and

A

B

Fig. 12.2. A. Ropes crossed ready for a run and a roundoff to a backward somersault. B. Using the twisting belt for roundoff backward somersault.

the bent-knee, flat-footed landing in the backward leaning position are like those for the backward handspring series (Fig. 12.1). Likewise, the push-away of the snap down part of the roundoff and the following backward armswing into the backward handspring are nearly identical to those between units in the series of backward handsprings. There should be an attempt to make the roundoff and the backward handspring all one continuous movement with the emphasis on the snap down portion of the roundoff. The handstand jerk to backward handspring is a good preliminary because it is more easily spotted than the roundoff to backward handspring.

If a safety belt is used for learning, either the ropes will have to be wrapped across the body at the start (Fig. 12.2A) in order to be correct after the roundoff, or a "twisting belt" will have to be used (Fig. 12.2B). Hand spotting should be sufficient if the parts and preliminaries have been well learned before attempting the combination and if the spotter is experienced.

12.3. Backward Handspring, Step Out. This variation differs from the normal backward handspring in that the handstand landing midway in the stunt is accompanied by a split, or fore and aft spreading of the straight legs (Fig. 12.3), and then, instead of a snap down, the comedown to the feet is with one foot at a time like the second half of a cartwheel or a step-down from a momentary handstand. Another variety of the step-out would be with a half twist of the hips executed during the step-out, so that the performer finishes his step-out facing the opposite direction. These back-

Fig. 12.3. Leg separation for backward handspring to step out.

ward handspring step-outs can be done from a handstand jerk, from a roundoff, or at the end of a series as well as from a standing start.

12.4. Cradle. A cradle on the mats has the appearance of half of a backward handspring to a landing on the hands and back of the neck and shoulders with a subsequent reversal of direction returning to the feet. The start is much like that of a backward handspring. The strong arm swing and body action are the same, the leg spring is about half as strong as for a backward handspring, and the head does not go back to see the landing area. The hands should land on the floor pointing outward and should be located a little farther apart than shoulder width. The arms catch the weight and yield with control, lowering the back of the shoulders to the mat as the body position changes from the arch that accompanies the original throw, to a piked position as the shoulders approach the mat. The recovery to the feet then is a snap up (see Stunt No. 7) preferably to a lay-out landing (see Stunt No. 7.4). The cradle can also be learned to a piked headstand with a headspring-type recovery to the feet. This "head cradle" demands a sure and strong catch with the hands and shock-absorbing lowering to the head, but is a most impressive movement for Floor Exercise.

Stunt No. 13—BACKWARD SOMERSAULT (Tucked)

DESCRIPTION OF ACTION

From a standing start, draw the straight arms backward while raising the heels without bending the knees (Fig. 13A). From this high-on-the-toes, arms-cocked position, the vigorous action begins. The arms swing forward and then to overhead with a free, fast, full arm swing. With this arm swing the heels drop to the mat, the knees bend a few degrees (10° to 20°) and then straighten quickly and forcefully, the ankles extend, and the feet press to effect a maximum-lift spring from the mat (Fig. 13B). As the body goes into the air and the arms swing into an upward and back-over stretch reach, the head is thrown backward forcefully. This puts the hips momentarily into the forward thrust position and the body into an arch or hyperextended position (Fig. 13B). Almost immediately after the feet leave the mat, there is a strenuous effort from both ends to get into the tuck position. The knees are bent, the waist is bent, and the arms come down to grasp the middle of the shins and pull the tuck together, and pull the legs around under the body (Fig. 13C). The brief tuck is followed by a release and opening action to a stand. The landing should be bent knee and usually to whole-foot rather than ball-of-the-foot contact with the mat (Fig. 13D).

STEPS IN LEARNING

1. The standing backward somersault requires better than average standing spring, good muscle tone in legs and abdomen, and some background in

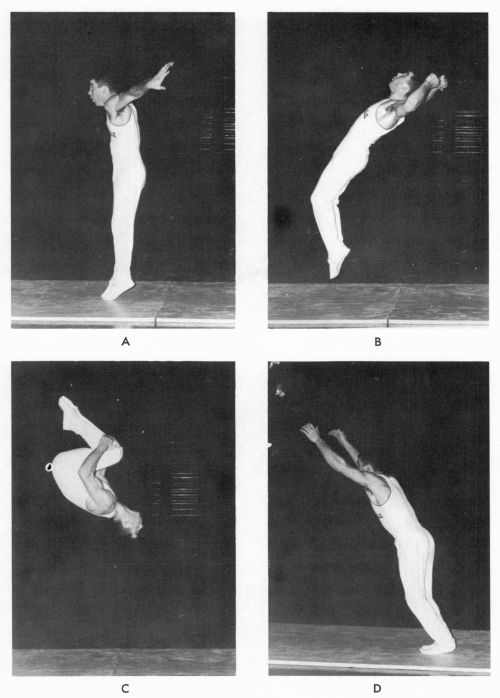

Fig. 13. Backward Somersault. A. Preparation for the spring. B. Throwing head and arms back and hips forward. C. Speeding up the spin with tight tuck. D. Open again for the landing.

Fig. 13E. Using the overhead suspension safety belt for learning backward somersault.

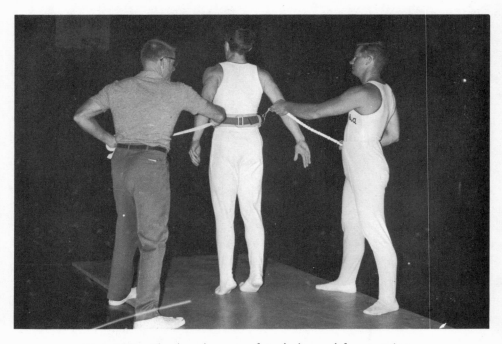

Fig. 13F. The hand-rope safety belt used for spotting.

the elementary tumbling skills including, of course, backward rolls.

2. The takeoff action to a vigorous spring with overhead arm reach, but without either the head throw, the back-over arm swing, or the tuck, should be practiced to the point of overlearning to facilitate a strong, confident spring when trying the whole stunt.

3. Another preliminary exercise to acquire the quick and accurate change from stretch to tuck can be done while lying flat on the back on the mat. Start with arms overhead, body outstretched in supine position, head back looking at hands. As suddenly, accurately, and completely as possible come to the hands-on-mid-shins, knees-on-chest, heels-against-buttocks, head-back position that should characterize the backward somersault tuck. Open out again and repeat this tuck practice exercise many times.

4. The next step in learning is an almost full-speed and full-scale attempt at the entire stunt as described above under "Description of Action," but with plenty of protective spotting by teacher or fellow students. The best spotting device is the overhead suspended belt, which can be handled by one spotter (Fig. 13E). The next best is a safety belt with hand ropes, which is manned by two assistants (Fig. 13F). Sometimes a towel around the waist with both ends gathered into the hands of one spotter or two towels held by two spotters can be used as a satisfactory substitute for a belt. If two spotters without towels or belt are used, they should face each other, one on each side of the performer, grasp the performer's clothing near his waist with the hands nearest his backside, and use the other hands (the ones nearest the performer's front side) to move in under his hips and boost him over. The grip on the clothing should be in a rotated position so that it will be in the strongest supporting grip during the latter part of the somersault when it is most needed (Fig. 13G). During the first attempts

Fig. 13G. Spotting the backward somersault without belt.

the performer should be reminded of the importance of opening late to a bent-knees, whole-foot landing. This will help protect his ankles, which are in jeopardy when the opening is too strong, too soon, and to a straight-knees, on-the-toes landing.

5. Spotting can become less strong and less helpful as technique becomes better until only a reach-in touch-lift is needed and eventually no spotting whatever.

CORRECTION OF ERRORS

A. Lack of sufficient height may be due to a native lack of leg spring or to a correctable error. Errors to look for to correct this fault are too deep a knee bend for the spring, poor coordination of arm swing and leg swing, insufficient overhead reach with the arms, and too much backward lean in the takeoff. Any one of these, or any combination of them, will detract from the height attained. In addition, the performer should be sure that he is exerting a maximum-speed and maximum-force effort including the final press away with the feet. Overlearning of Step 2 of "Steps in Learning" described above will help insure maximum attainable height.

B. Lack of sufficient rotation may, in some cases, be attributable simply to lack of height as discussed just above, but may occur even when sufficient height has been obtained because of a too *slow* rotation. Fast rotation is secured by the backward throw of the head and backward overhead swing of the arms, by the forward hip thrust that accompanies the takeoff spring, and particularly by the quick and complete compacting of the body into the tucked position soon after takeoff. The arm swing and head throw can be practiced in a standing position without springing, and the tuck can be practiced in the supine position as described in "Steps in Learning," Step 3. Good abdominal strength and arm pull must be developed in order to facilitate the process of pulling into a tuck against the centrifugal force of rotation.

C. Opening out of the tuck too soon, or too completely, may result in under-spinning and failure to land on the feet as a result. This underturning and especially a too forceful complete leg straightening when a little under-turned may result in foot, ankle, or knee injury. The tuck should be held late, the feet pulled around under the body with the arm pull, and the opening should be to a bent-knee somewhat flat-footed landing (especially in the learning phases). It is better to overturn than underturn when learning.

VARIATIONS AND COMBINATIONS

13.1. Tucked Backward Somersault from Roundoff. The roundoff for this combination is done with good running speed, a forceful execution, and a strong snap down to a practically straight-knee, ball-of-the-foot landing with immediate bounce takeoff into the backward somersault lift. The succeeding backward somersault differs from the standing backward somersault in several important ways. The arm lift is more vertical and less

Fig. 13.1. Using the traveling overhead suspension twisting belt for round-off backward somersault.

back-over than that for the standing back. The head does not throw back immediately, but continues to look forward until the peak of the lift. The stretch position is more prolonged with the tuck starting after the stretch and as the delayed head throws backward. These differences are present mainly because of the added height created by the incoming momentum from the run and roundoff converted by the bounce takeoff into upward force. To get this added height, not only incoming speed is necessary, but also good push against the mat with the arms followed by overhead reach and the putting of the feet down at a considerable distance from where the hands left the mat so that the body angle at the time of bounce off the toes is a little forward leaning or vertical, but not backward leaning.

The best spotting for this and similar and more difficult tumbling is a twisting belt suspended from overhead by ropes from blocks on pulley wheels running along horizontal cables above the tumbling mat (Fig. 13.1). Satisfactory protection can be given with an ordinary belt with ropes (Fig. 12.2A) using two agile and experienced spotters. The ropes are crossed (one in front and one behind) before starting to allow for the roundoff (unless a "twisting belt" is used), and the spotters must run along with the performer during his approach and roundoff. A learner should try this with free spotting (no belt) only if he can consistently do it with the belt on and no assistance or has a very experienced and competent spotter.

13.2. Tucked Backward Somersault from Backward Handspring.   This combination would usually be done with at least a preceding roundoff to add speed. It can be done with merely a standing start, but would lack the height and beauty the added momentum would give it. Other stunts may follow the roundoff before the backward handspring backward somersault, especially other backward handsprings. The transition from the final backward handspring to the tucked backward somersault, and the somersault itself are practically identical to the transition from the roundoff to the tucked backward somersault described above for Stunt No. 13.1. One point needs emphasis here, however, and that is that a lower than normal backward handspring to a more bent-arm landing on the hands and an emphasis on the arm push for the snap down are helpful on the last backward handspring before a high backward somersault, tucked or open. Learning this one safely requires the same spotting techniques described for Stunt No. 13.1 above.

13.3. Open Backward Somersault.   The open backward somersault can be executed from a standing start or with momentum gained from a run and roundoff with or without interceding backward handsprings. There is the high open backward somersault, commonly called a layout (Fig. 13.3), which is done from a high-on-the-ball-of-the-foot bounce takeoff similar to the tuck backward somersault takeoff, and there is the low open backward somersault commonly called a whip-over, done from a more backward leaning, less bouncy, lower-heel type of takeoff (Figs 13.4 and 13.5). In both cases the head is immediately thrown completely backward and the hips are thrown forward into an arched or hyperextended position that is held all the way to the landing in case of the layout back, but modified late in the rotation to a bent-at-the-waist landing position in case of the whip-over (either standing or from a run and roundoff, etc.). The arms are kept either down along the sides or out perpendicular to the body in a swan position after the short lifting action in the high layout backward somersault. The arms are kept in close to the trunk, usually in a bent-arm position after the initial throws in most whip-overs. An exception to this arm position is seen in the open backward somersault preceding a backward handspring, which is the next variation described below.

13.4. Open Backward Somersault Followed by a Backward Handspring. The technique for the open backward somersault when it is followed by a backward handspring is different in two ways. The most obvious, perhaps, is that it should be overturned a little farther than usual with the landing on the whole foot in a backward leaning position. This is assuming, of course, that the backward handspring throw will begin immediately as it should for maximum speed and continuity. The other difference is less obvious, but extremely helpful. The arms on the somersault throw should swing way back overhead in an extended position as if the tumbler were going to do a backward handspring (Fig. 13.4). The armswing

Fig. 13.3. The layout backward somersault.

Fig. 13.4. The throw for the low open backward somersault to be followed by a backward handspring.

Fig. 13.5. The throw for the low open backward somersault to be followed by one or more similar somersaults.

reaches its limit at a point a foot or so above the mat level and the arms remain more or less at this extended, hands-toward-the-mat, vertical position while the body changes from arched to bent, the feet land flat with bent knees and a backward body lean. Then, as the tumbler springs into the backward handspring, his arms swing again, straight and free and forcefully all the way back to the landing on the mat, which is the midpoint of the backward handspring. This extended arm action in the whip-over somersault makes the somersault itself more difficult so that it requires a stronger bounce and a stronger whip into it to be sure to overturn the landing, but this extra effort is well repaid by the greater speed and continuity that can be added to the transition between the somersault and backward handspring and the resulting speed and force for the rest of the sequence. Alternating backward handsprings and backward somersaults can thus be done with such speed and continuity that the series almost has the appearance of a fast series of backward handsprings.

13.5. Open Backward Somersault Series (Back Bounders). When the performer is doing one backward somersault after another, the takeoff for each should be a bounce from the balls of the feet with heels nearly touching or barely touching the mat. The arm, head, and body throw should be forcefully executed into a full, body-arched, head-back position. At this point, after the eyes spot the mat, the body bends as much as is necessary to bring the feet into landing position under the body ready for another bounce takeoff ino another somersault.

As compared to the open backward somersault before a backward handspring, some differences should be noted. The arms do not swing in the fully extended position but swing back strongly in a slightly bent arm position (Fig. 13.5) and quickly change to a more bent position as contrasted to the prolonged straight-armed position in Stunt No. 13.4. The landing of the somersault, when followed by another somersault, is less overturned, less bent knee and less heels down on the mat than when followed by the backward handspring. In both sequences the somersault should be low and fast, but it is not as low for bounders as it is for alternating backward whip-overs and backward handsprings.

5

Floor Exercise

USE OF TUMBLING IN THE FLOOR EXERCISE EVENT

The internationally contested gymnastic event that is most closely related to tumbling is Floor Exercise. This event is part of the Olympic Games program in Gymnastics, and as such is an integral part of gymnastics competition all over the world. The chief ingredient of a competitive floor exercise is tumbling. Therefore, almost all of the material presented in the preceding chapters is usable in Floor Exercise.

Two important qualities of the performing area for floor exercise as compared to that usually provided for the tumbling event modify and limit the tumbling used in the floor exercise event. The space is both shorter and harder than that used in the tumbling event. These characteristics put a premium on the short strong run or approach and on movements that can be done without any run. They also tend toward short sequences or single stunts and away from those where reasonable comfort or safety demands thick padding on the takeoff or landing surface. These limitations are only relative, however, as stunts of high difficulty and tumbling sequences of five or six stunts are occasionally seen in high-level floor exercise routines.

Floor exercise tumbling differs in some other ways from the Tumbling event because of the characteristics, traditions, and governing rules of the event. Form, style, and grace including lightness afoot are much more important elements in competitive floor exercise than in competitive tumbling, and are to be emphasized more than intrinsic difficulty. Floor exercise form includes small details of hand extension, finger closing, body posture, finely balanced landings to a static position, or controlled flowing movement into the next part of the sequence.

COMPOSITION AND SPECIFICATIONS OF THE FLOOR EXERCISE

There are three primary ingredients in a good floor exercise other than tumbling agility. One of these is balance, primarily inverted balance.

Variations of the hand balance including different ways of getting into it and out of it and, in advanced routines, the one-hand balance are the most common ways of demonstrating the balance element, although variations of a one-foot balance (scales) are also used.

Another essential ingredient of the men's floor exercise event is strength. Power is most often shown with variations of the press to handstand and, in more advanced routines, by one or another kind of plange (horizontal handstand).

The third element in floor exercise, in addition to tumbling, is flexibility. Suppleness is most often demonstrated with splits, limbers, and scales. It is often combined into a tumbling, balance, or strength movement, but whether it is separate or combined, suppleness must be demonstrated in the execution of a well-rounded floor exercise.

The floor exercise is performed within a 13 meter (39.37 foot) square area. Although it is sometimes performed on the bare wooden floor, it should be done on a thin, firm, and resilient mat surface. Appropriate mats of sufficient size are expensive, however, and various substitutes including the floor itself are in common use. When the performers do not have the desirable protection of mats, they should be protected against bruising of the feet by wearing effective sponge-type plastic insoles inside their gymnastic shoes.

The competitors in this event must perform their sequence within a time limit, and are penalized for using more or less than the prescribed time. The routine must be at least 50 seconds and not more than 70 seconds in length. The performer should use virtually all segments of his area traversing it crosswise and diagonally in several directions. His routine should be an intermixture of the four elements: tumbling, balance, strength, and flexibility, with the major portion being tumbling. The sequence should be a continuous flowing from one part to the next. The only legitimate pauses are the brief holding of the balances and occasionally of a flexibility position. The whole should be a visually pleasing, rhythmic (with changes of pace) composition with a premium on originality and ingenuity.

In actual practice the floor exercise as seen in competition often does show more variety and differences between competitors than are shown in other gymnastic events. There is less tendency to direct imitation and stereotype routines. Even when all required elements are included, there is still room for difference of emphasis with some gymnasts emphasizing flexibility, others balance, others strength, with a minimum of one or both of the other two. Tumbling, however, is a substantial part of the routines of all successful floor exercise gymnasts. The good tumbler who can develop a reasonable ability in balance, strength, and flexibility is more likely to succeed than the limber artist, strongman, or balance expert who is weak in tumbling.

SOME NONTUMBLING FLOOR EXERCISE SKILLS

Following is a selection of a few skills and variations that have not been touched upon in the tumbling portion of the book but that are common ways of demonstrating the balance, strength, and flexibility elements in Free Exercise. This is by no means a comprehensive presentation and the examples of skills vary considerably in difficulty. It is hoped that it may point the way toward some more of the hundreds of movements and positions that are appropriate for Floor Exercise.

Stunt No. 14—SWEDISH FALL

This movement is a very simple, but eye-pleasing one that often serves to terminate a series of faster moving parts, supply a short pause, and lead into the next sequence. The simple fall itself consists of falling forward with straight body and splitting legs to a catch with the hands and one foot on the floor and the other foot as high up backward as it can reach without bending either knee (demonstrating flexibility). Immediately after the hands hit the floor, the arms bend to lower the face to the floor (Fig. 14). Added interest can be inserted by starting the initial fall backward and turning over during the early part of the fall to make the catch as indicated above. Other varieties involve full or double twists during the forward starting fall. The fall is often followed by a half turn to a split or sit on the mat.

Fig. 14. Swedish Fall.

Stunt No. 15—SINGLE-LEG CIRCLES

Start from a crouched position with the hands on the mat forward of the feet and one leg extended backward with pointed foot. If the right leg is back, it circles forward in a counterclockwise circle under the right hand, then the left (Fig. 15A), and then the left foot (Fig. 15B) to return to its starting position (Fig. 15C). This is accomplished by shifting the weight in order to lift the appropriate member as the circling leg approaches it. The circle should be smooth with straight leg and pointed foot and be free of contact of the circling leg with the floor at all times. Two or three circles should be sufficient to show continuity.

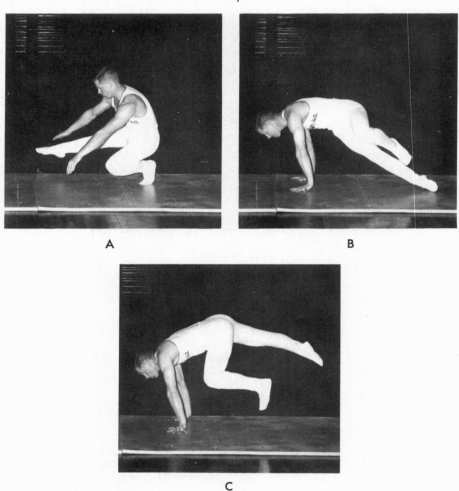

A

B

C

Fig. 15. Single-leg Circles. A. Swinging-leg circles forward under the hands. B. Leg continues around as other leg jumps over. C. Ready to start a second counterclockwise circle.

Stunt No. 16—SCALES

The most common and possibly the best looking scale is done in a swan position. From a stand, the performer shifts his weight onto one foot, bends forward at the waist spreading his arms into the horizontal position, and, at the same time, raises the free leg backward upward to above the horizontal plane without bending either leg. This position (Fig. 16A) is held for a few seconds to demonstrate balance and flexibility. Other ways of getting into the scale would include moving into it from a backward limber, from a backward handspring step-out (see Stunt No. 12.3), and from a forward walk-over (see Stunt No. 9.5), or a tinsica (see Stunt No. 9.3). One variation of the scale position involves extending the arm corresponding to the horizontal leg backward tightly against the body and leg, and the other arm horizontally forward overhead (Fig. 16B). A more difficult

A

B

Fig. 16. A. The swan scale. B. Forward reaching scale. *(Continued on page 92.)*

Fig. 16. *Continued.*   C. Side scale.

variation, called a side scale, requires the same position as just described except that the head and body are turned 90° to face one wall instead of the floor (Fig. 16C).

Stunt No. 17—SPLITS

Like the preceding three stunts, but to a greater extent, the splits require flexibility. The tendons and ligaments in the crotch area can be slowly and gradually lengthened by various stretching exercises done regularly (and somewhat painfully) over a period of months or years. The ordinary splits with one leg forward and one backward is the easiest variety (Fig. 17A). A position part way down with hands supporting part of the weight is a common learning position from which stretching can be accomplished under control. Splits should be approached gradually with plenty of warm-up to prevent injury. The lateral splits (Japanese splits) are much more difficult, requiring more flexibility to extend the legs laterally, one to each side, and lower the crotch to the mat (Fig. 17B). Many years of intense flexibility exercise, especially the incomplete splits itself, are necessary for most gymnasts to acquire this position. Splits can be stepped into, slid into, or jumped into, or they can be a landing position from tumbling stunts such as backward handspring or backward somersault. When the split is used as a landing position from a tumbling stunt or jump, the landing is really made in a partial split with an immediate sliding-lowering to the complete position.

Two other split-type flexibility positions can appropriately be mentioned here. The standing vertical split involves raising one leg high, grasping and holding it in position with the hand (Fig. 17C). The second position could be called the pancake split. It is done by sitting on the mat with legs

Fig. 17. A. Ordinary splits. B. Lateral (Japanese) splits. C. Standing vertical splits. *(Continued on page 94.)*

Fig. 17. *Continued.*   **D. Pancake splits.**

spread laterally until nearly parallel, then the hands reach out to the feet and the body is bent forward to place the chest and chin on the mat also (Fig. 17D).

Stunt No. 18—STRADDLE JUMPS

Leap or bounce from both feet straight up as high as possible. As soon as the feet leave the floor, they start spreading toward a lateral split or straddle position. The knees are kept straight, the feet pointed, and the legs are spread and lifted as high as the performer is able. The arms extend along the legs to reach the front of the pointed feet at the height of the jump (Fig. 18A). An alternative position for the arms at the height of the lift which is also very effective is the extension of the arms straight downward between the legs parallel to each other (Fig. 18B). Agility and flexibility can be demonstrated with straddle jumps.

Stunt No. 19—PRESS TO HANDSTAND

One of the less difficult usable presses to handstand is the tuck press. Starting from a squat position on both feet with hands shoulder width apart and close to the feet, the weight is taken onto the hands and arms by leaning forward, with face toward the mat, bending the arms while keeping as close a tuck as possible until the feet come off the floor. Now, with muscular strength slowly rotate the body, getting the hips above the shoulders (Fig. 19A). Next, slowly open from bent waist to straight body and from bent knees to straight knees, at the same time straightening the arms to a handstand. This is done slowly and deliberately without snap or sudden movement. A fairly "solid" handstand (see Stunt No. 4.5) and good arm strength are necessary preliminaries. Vertical push-ups (in handstand with feet against wall) and the press-down (from handstand slowly to squat

A

B

Fig. 18. A. Straddle jump with arms extended laterally. B. Straddle jump with arms extended downward.

position, i.e., the reverse of the press to handstand) are recommended strength-building exercises.

A somewhat more difficult press to handstand is the piked press. To start this press, bend forward at the waist with straight legs from a standing position to place the hands on the floor 20 to 30 inches in front of the feet, shoulder-width apart. Shift the weight forward onto the hands by bending the arms and moving the face forward and closer to the floor (Fig. 19B). With the face still several inches from the floor check the arm-bending and maintain the elbow angle at the acquired angle while lifting the hips so that the feet are lifted from the mat. The body then slowly straightens as do the arms to the handstand position. The tucked press-up (Fig. 19A) and the piked press-down (Fig. 19B in reverse) are good preparations.

Another excellent press is the straight-arm, straight-leg press to handstand (stiff-stiff). This one is similar to the piked press to handstand (Fig. 19B) but is done without bending the arms. The prerequisites to learning it are excellent forward-bending flexibility, and competence in the easier press-ups (Figs. 19A and 19B). The hands are placed very close to the feet instead of 20 to 30 inches forward as in the bent-arm press. After the weight is taken onto the hands and the feet leave the mat, the trunk is brought into a vertical position or past before the body moves from the piked into the straight position by raising the straight legs from the waist. The stiff-stiff press down and the straddle stiff-stiff (Fig. 19C) are useful preparations.

One of the most difficult presses is the straight-body press from prone to handstand. The starting position is lying face down on the mat with the body hyperextended (arched), and the hands on the mat beside the hips. From here starts the downward pressure of the hands which raises the body, feet end highest, from the mat (Fig. 19D). As the feet go up the shoulders move back toward the hands. When the body attains an angle of 60 or 70 degrees with the mat, the arms start to straighten. The arms complete their extension as the body reaches the vertical position of the handstand. In the learning phases a rocking action in the prone arched position will make for a simpler press until strength is acquired to do it properly. Coming from the handstand slowly down to the prone position by shifting the shoulders forward is another good learning device.

ADDITIONAL POSITION AND MOVEMENTS

There are many, many more Floor Exercise movements and positions in common usage that have not been described above. There are even more I am sure that will be devised and put into action by creative gymnasts in the years to come. It is hoped that what has been presented will provide a basis and a stimulus for imitative and creative learning by aspiring gymnasts.

Fig. 19. A. Tuck press to handstand. B. Piked press to handstand. C. The straddle straight-arm straight-leg press to handstand. D. The straight-body press to handstand.